STICKMAKING
The Complete Guide

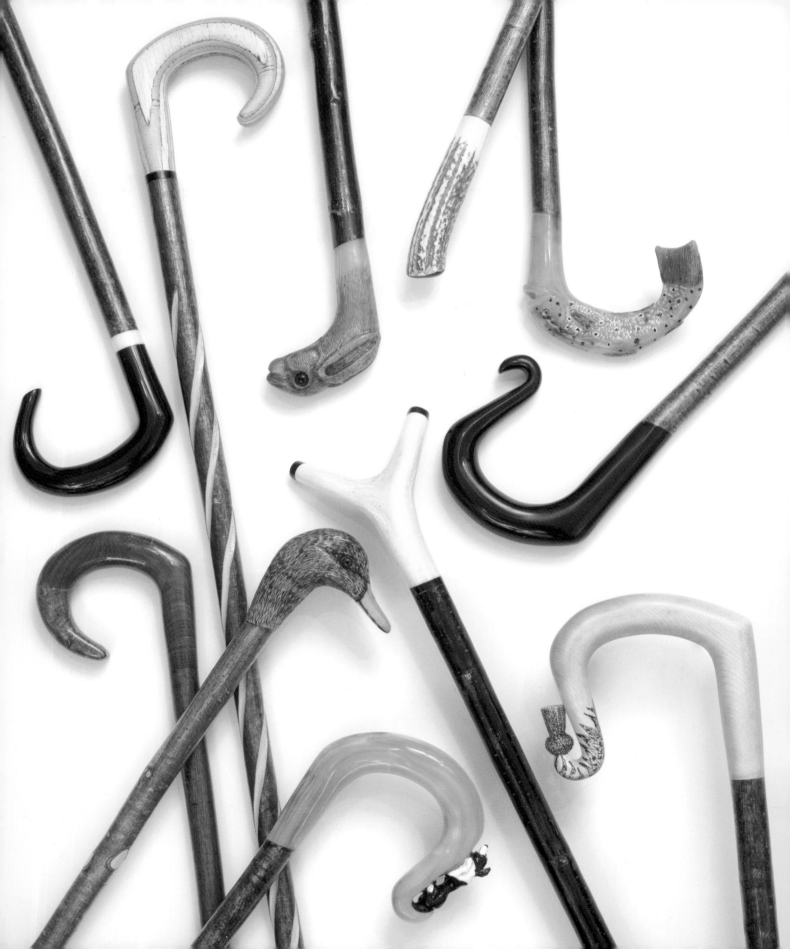

STICKMAKING
The Complete Guide

CHARLIE WALKER

THE CROWOOD PRESS

First published in 2018 by
The Crowood Press Ltd
Ramsbury, Marlborough
Wiltshire SN8 2HR

www.crowood.com

© Charlie Walker 2018

British Library Cataloguing-in-Publication Data
A catalogue record for this book is available from the British Library.

ISBN 978 1 78500 413 1

Frontispiece: Colin Mills

Typeset by Sharon Dainton.
Printed and bound in India by Parksons Graphics

Contents

Introduction

I have been very fortunate to receive a lot of help from stickmakers around the UK who have willingly given me their advice, time and encouragement. In this book, it is my intention to pass on some of the information that I have gained about stickmaking to any reader who is interested in this absorbing pastime and would like to make a range of walking or working sticks using different materials and techniques.

The book provides extensive advice and information about the materials, equipment and tools required to make a variety of sticks from timber, antler and horn. The early chapters provide general information about stick types and shapes, advice on tools and equipment and where and how to get ideas and inspiration on stickmaking. The book continues with a list of timbers that are often used for stickmaking. Many stickmakers prefer to collect their own timber to make handles and shanks; guidance is given on cutting and collecting green timber and methods of storing and protecting the timber from pests. A chapter is dedicated to straightening shanks; it describes how to make simple jigs and equipment to enable bent sticks to be straightened. One of the most important aspects of making good-quality walking and working sticks is creating strong and reliable joints between the handle and shank, but the most essential part is fitting a ferrule onto the tip that will protect the stick for many years. Several jointing methods are detailed which will provide the reader with some options for making first-class joints for various types of sticks.

There are several projects for the reader to work on using step-by-step guides that describe the processes and techniques used, which are supported by numerous photographs. Each stickmaking chapter begins by making plain versions and progresses through to making more complex sticks, culminating in using a variety of methods to decorate and enhance the sticks. In order to avoid too much duplication, some of the repetitive steps required when making the featured sticks have been avoided; however most of the techniques and methods that I use are included within the various projects featured throughout the book.

Some guidance is given on exhibiting and competing in club and national competitions and gives pointers to some aspects an experienced judge will be looking for in a prize-winning stick. The book concludes with a short tribute to one of the very best stickmakers I had the pleasure to know; Gordon Flintoft, and includes pictures of some of his excellent sticks.

Apart from Gordon, the sticks featured in this guide have been made by the author using the materials, tools and equipment described throughout the book.

The equipment and methods used here are based on tried and tested designs and methods that have been and continue to be used by many stickmakers throughout the country. Some stickmakers use different designs of presses to bulk sheep and cow horn that work well for them, others may use different manufacturers and types of tools. There is an abundance of tools, timbers, adhesives and finishing products to choose from, however stickmaking follows a few basic principles and methods that are described throughout the book. There is no right or wrong way of making a stick but there are expectations and standards we should all strive to maintain when making sticks for others to use.

I hope you enjoy your stickmaking and find the information in this book helpful.

Charlie Walker

LEFT: A plywood handle on spiral shank - Photo by Colin Mills

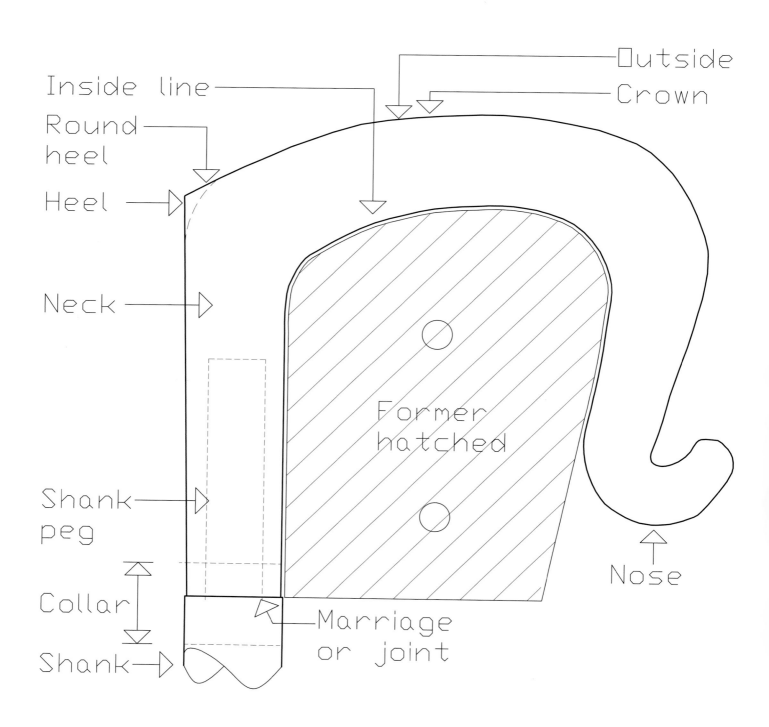

Inside line

Round heel

Heel

Neck

Shank peg

Collar

Shank

Outside

Crown

Former hatched

Marriage or joint

Nose

Chapter 1
Fundamental Information

Two traditional types of handles that are regularly used in stickmaking are shown in the sketches; the first is a shepherd's crook shape and is often referred to as a 'nose-out' handle. The second shape is a 'nose-in' handle, used regularly for walking and commonly known as a market stick. Both the handles are drawn full size and the dimensions replicate a finished handle, enabling readers to make their own templates of the shapes. The sketches also include a hatched former reproducing the inside shape of the handles, which is useful for anyone wishing to bend and shape a horn. The parts identified in the sketches are used throughout the book to describe some of the steps used when making most styles of handles. The full-size patterns are intended to be used as guidelines for making handles; the finished size, appearance and shape of any handle is decided by the maker, who may well produce variations of the examples. The two most popular methods of fixing handles onto shanks are shown in the sketches; the first is using a joint cut directly onto a shank, which is commonly called a peg or dowel joint, and the second is a stud joint using threaded rod; both these joints are featured in the book. Shepherd's crooks are often joined onto a shank using an angled joint rather than a flat joint. The reason an angled joint is used is that it is less prone to twisting on a shank when used as a working crook to catch and hold a sheep. Examples of angled joints are shown in later chapters. Other jointing methods that allow stick handles to be removed or replaced are also included in later chapters. A very important joint is the one used to fit a ferrule on the tip of the shank to protect the stick from abnormal wear and tear and is described in detail later.

Collars are used between the handle and shank for two principal reasons; the first is to strengthen this crucial joint and the second is to provide a means of decorating a stick. Collars can be made from horn, timber and metals such as brass, nickel or silver. A well-fitted collar can satisfy both of the principal purposes of strength and decoration. The ideal position when fitting a collar to strengthen the joint is shown on the sketch. Occasionally decorative collars are added after the stick is made, the collar is simply slipped up the shank until it is a tight fit onto the handle or shank; this method is not recommended. Strong, close-fitting joints are one of the most important aspects of making good-quality and serviceable sticks.

Traditional-shaped handles are generally made with a round or square heel and both types are shown in the sketches. There is a contradiction with a square heel as it should look square but feel round; in other words the heel must be comfortable to hold and use - avoid leaving a sharp, uncomfortable surface on the heel.

Older stickmaking books often refer to stick components and their size in inches; because we now live in the metric world a small conversion chart is shown below for reference, with some of the most common measurements used by stickmakers. Please note they are rounded to the nearest number; the tolerances quoted are acceptable.

$$5/_{64}in = 2mm$$
$$3/_{32}in = 2.4mm$$
$$1/_{8}in = 3mm$$
$$1/_{4}in = 6mm$$
$$5/_{16}in = 8mm$$
$$3/_{8}in = 10mm$$
$$1/_{2}in = 12mm$$
$$5/_{8}in = 16mm$$
$$1in = 25mm$$
$$1 5/_{8}in = 30mm$$
$$1 3/_{4}in = 32mm$$
$$2in = 50mm$$

Left: Sketch of a shepherd's crook

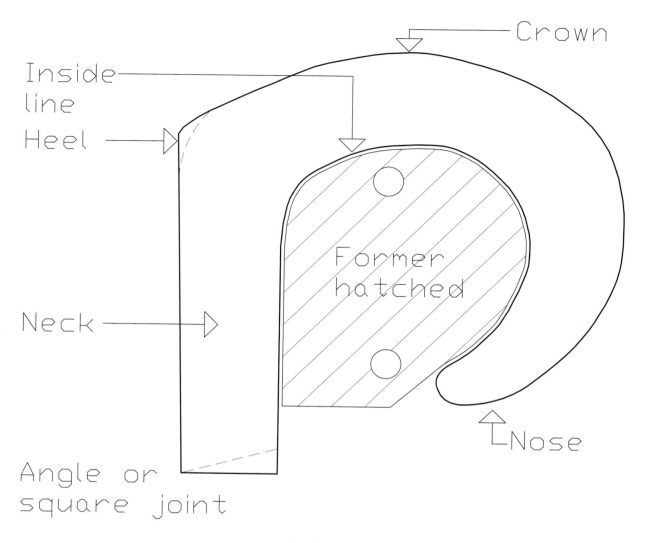

Sketch of a nose-in market stick.

6in = 150mm
12in = 305mm
24in = 610mm
36in = 915mm
48in = 1,220mm
52in = 1,320mm
60in = 1,525mm

There are very few exacting measurements used in stickmaking, although there are several guidelines as to the shape, size and appearance of different styles of sticks that have been established over many years. These principles are helpful to stickmakers in getting the correct ratio between the handles and shanks, so the appearance of a stick is in proportion and is an attractive shape. Too often sticks are made with their appearance being spoilt by inappropriate sizes and shapes being included, which makes the stick look unsightly and feel unbalanced, therefore difficult to use.

These characteristics are not as important in unconventional (sometimes referred to as novelty) sticks that are very popular; there is a considerable market for these interesting and unique sticks. The makers are not confined by the conventional standards and expectations that have developed over many years with traditional sticks. Many stickmakers prefer to make these as they allow the maker to use their imagination, flare, skill, dexterity and mastery to produce some amazing and stunning sticks that many people love to own. If you have the vision and talent to make unusual and interesting sticks, have a go and you will be surprised and encouraged by the amount of interest shown in them from inquisitive potential buyers.

People's choices vary considerably and they select sticks of different weights, heights, styles and sizes for personal reasons. Never assume what type of stick an individual will choose; often people will seek your advice on what height, weight and style of stick will suit them best for their particular circumstances or interests. Be prepared to give guidance on the best stick for them, explain the advantages and disadvantages of the different types of sticks you have available. Here are two examples I have encountered while displaying sticks in local fairs. A petite lady selected a tall, heavy thumb stick, which seemed far too big for her size; however, she explained it was required to support a branch of a fruit tree that was laden with pears! Another person wanted a stick of a particular length so it would fit across the boot of the car; the type and price of the stick wasn't a major concern as long as it would fit behind the seats in the car boot. If you intend to make sticks to sell, make a selection of sticks so there is plenty of choice for any potential customers and be prepared to negotiate the cost and modify the length of a selected stick.

Sticks and canes became extremely popular and fashionable around the turn of the twentieth century; almost everyone carried a stick wherever they went. Poorer people would use a simply made wooden stick while the wealthiest would have several sticks and canes made from exotic woods, with elegant carved handles made from precious materials. Some sticks contained swords and guns while others would have a small container for the owner's favourite tipple. It was around this period when unconventional and novelty sticks

became very popular and different materials were used extensively to make magnificent and well-crafted sticks and canes. Large stickmaking companies employed hundreds of workers and a few produced catalogues of their extensive range of sticks. These old catalogues are very interesting and informative, as they show many examples of types and styles. A fascinating example is the crook; there are several shapes of handles displayed including a Brighton crook, a round heel crook, a Tam O'Shanter crook, a square heel crook, and a leg cleek. The crooks also have several types of noses such as a half-curled nose, a curled nose, a looped nose and a decorated nose.

There were many styles and types of walking sticks and canes made during this era demonstrating how many variations are possible in stickmaking, which is why it is impracticable to set precise measurements for the many variations of just one style. The period during and after the First World War resulted in the rapid decline of owning trendy and expensive sticks; many workers lost their jobs as large stickmaking companies closed. A few independent skilled workers continued making basic walking and working sticks. Following the Second World War, as people have become wealthier, the demand for well-made traditional and unorthodox sticks has steadily increased and there are a few professional stickmakers selling their work. Also an increasing number of people have taken up the absorbing hobby of stickmaking. Sticks have been and continue to be used as an aid for walking; such a stick must be strong enough to support the user and be cut to the correct height.

People who enjoy hiking will often use a tall stick for support while climbing or descending steep slopes and pathways, or for testing the ground conditions. Sticks are a useful aid when

walking along overgrown paths and tracks, as they can be used to knock down stinging nettles, thistles and thorns. Shepherds and farmers often use sticks when herding sheep or cattle; beaters use sticks to test the ground conditions and tap trees to raise game birds for shooters. Fishermen and bailiffs will often use a stick to test the depth of water and check the bottom of the lake or river to ensure it is safe.

There are several institutions and organizations that use sticks in their workplace or business; some are based on tradition and others are a requirement. Military officers and personnel carry various styles and types of sticks especially when participating in formal pageants and parades. Mining deputies traditionally used sticks a yard long to measure progress and test the surrounding conditions of the mine. In the early days of railways, track inspectors used sticks to check that the distance between rail tracks was correct. Sticks are used by tribal leaders as a sign of their authority and are often decorated with symbols. Senior clergy frequently carry a crozier as a sign of their position, which is usually in the form of a crook with religious decorations built into the handle.

Working shepherds will often choose an uncomplicated, plain stick for everyday use and will use a more expensive, elaborate stick when attending shows and sheepdog trials. Shepherds and farmers choose different sizes and shapes of working sticks and crooks depending on the breed of cattle and sheep and the type of terrain they have to contend with on a regular basis. Countryside workers such as bailiffs, stewards, gamekeepers, forestry and estate managers regularly use sticks as aids when working or traversing the land – again, their choice and style of stick will vary considerably. Pig breeders can be seen at shows using a 'stockmans' stick in conjunction with a board to move the pig from the pens into the show ring and back again following the judging. These examples demonstrate the diversity of stickmaking and indicate why there are so few hard and fast dimensions.

Despite the lack of precise measurements, several guidelines and standards have developed over time and should be considered when making a traditional walking or working stick. Some generally acceptable standards are: The width of a gape of a crook is

about four fingers, which is approximately 90mm ($3^1/_2$ in). The nose should be about 10–12mm ($^1/_2$ in) above the joint line. The inside line of the heel should be a continuation of the inside line of the shank. The outside line of the heel may very gently slope

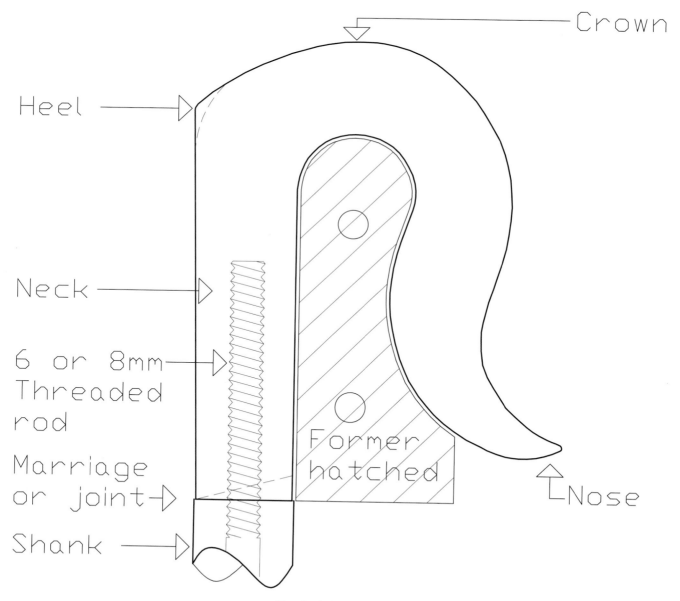

Sketch of a leg cleek.

outwards. These details may seem insignificant, but they help to improve the appearance of a handle by giving the impression that the handle stands up rather than drooping towards the nose. Protrusions or decorations should not interfere with the functionality of regularly used walking or working sticks, therefore avoid carving an object onto the crown or heel that will interfere with the viability of these working sticks. Carving letters into a handle (for example a name) or inserting an object so it doesn't protrude is acceptable, as it does not interfere with the practicality of the stick. Notwithstanding, carvings that protrude can be made on the crown of taller staffs and sticks that are normally held by the neck or shank, as they do not hamper the use of the stick.

Shanks of traditional sticks should be perfectly straight, bends and kinks are not acceptable in exhibition sticks. It is also important that a shank is in keeping with the type and style of handle, the complete stick should feel balanced in the hand. A parallel shank on a crook improves the balance of the stick better than a shank with a severe taper when used in its working position (held by the handle). Short, light-handled walking sticks are more suited to a tapered shank. Avoid using timber that is too springy on shanks; a shank must feel firm and have sufficient strength to provide adequate support for the user. Joints should be strong and close fitting. The complete stick should have a smooth and durable finish. Generally the handle must be in perfect line with the shank when viewed from either the nose or the heel; an exception to this is a leaping trout handle where the tail is curved. Complying with these traditional guidelines will enhance both the appearance and the feel of most sticks. A working shepherd is very particular as to the size, weight, balance, strength and appearance of a crook and it may take

some time to choose the stick that is most suitable for their particular environment and breed of sheep.

A leg cleek is a term used for smaller and lighter crooks. Their handles are shaped with a tighter gape than a full crook and the shanks are often shorter than a standard crook. Shepherds use them to catch sheep and lambs by their legs; they are often used to separate an individual sheep or lamb from a flock of enclosed sheep in a pen, which is why some shepherds prefer to use a shorter shank in an enclosed area. They have to be used carefully as twisting the stick can result in breaking a lamb's leg as it tries to escape.

Poultry farmers also use leg cleeks to catch poultry such as geese and turkeys by their necks. Leg cleeks are the only sticks to have set measurements for the handle and not all shepherds agree with these sizes; some believe the mouth is too small. The traditional measurement used for the mouth (gape) is an old half penny, and for the inside of the crown loop it is an old penny. These equate to 25mm (1 inch) for the mouth and 30mm ($1^1/_4$ inches) for the inside of the loop; some judges continue to use these sizes when examining show sticks.

Commercially made aluminium leg cleeks are regularly used as working sticks and their measurements have a mouth and loop of the same size which is 27mm ($1^1/_8$ inches). Again, this highlights how measurements can vary in the same type of stick.

Stickmakers will often make sticks longer than normal to accommodate some clients who prefer them taller than a standard height, therefore ferrules are not always fitted until the stick is finally selected and the height agreed. A longer shank is easily shortened should a customer request a short stick, whereas it is often impractical to lengthen a shank.

If you make sticks to sell it is

advisable to have an adjustable version to help people choose their preferred height before finally cutting a shank to length and fitting a ferrule. It is especially helpful for people who want a shorter walking stick for support, the height is very important to the user who relies on a stick. When making walking or working sticks, it is most important that they feel balanced in the hand and are functional and comfortable to use; they must be well finished and have an excellent appearance. Some people will request a thick, heavy handle while others choose a lighter handle that they can grip with ease.

Everyone has a different interpretation of what makes a good conventional stick and even experienced show judges' opinions of sticks will differ, although they will all agree that certain standards must be achieved. Some requirements are that the stick must have a straight shank and a strong, neat joint; the shank and handle should be aligned; the handle and shank should be balanced and there must be no scratches, marks or defects on either. Decorations must be an accurate representation of the subject and be of a suitable scale. An excellent finish is essential. These are standards that all stickmakers should strive to achieve when making walking and working sticks, as they demonstrate that the maker is skilful and makes good-quality and reliable sticks. It is not necessary for unconventional or unorthodox sticks to fully meet all of the standards expected in traditional sticks, nevertheless it is important that the workmanship is of a high standard and features such as joints are neat and strong, there are no scratches or defects and the stick is well finished.

Having considered some of the fundamental information, decide on the type of sticks you wish to make and obtain some tools and equipment.

Chapter 2
Tools and Equipment

Some useful tools

Always try to obtain good-quality and reliable tools that will last for years. Several types of simple wooden sticks can be made with a few tools to begin your journey into this fascinating pastime. The following tools will get you started; a sharp retractable bladed knife, a couple of sharp carving knives, a small hand saw, a small hacksaw, a coping saw, a few different sizes and shapes of rasps, some carving chisels, a wooden mallet and a combination square with a ruler. A means of holding a stick while working on it is helpful; a portable vice that clamps onto a table or a Workmate or similar will get you started.

A suitable space

A most important requirement to make sticks or to carry out most hobbies is to have a suitable space to carry out the various tasks. This may range from a corner in a room, a small garden shed, conservatory, garage or a dedicated workshop, ideally that has lighting and a power supply available. The amount of space available will also determine the type of tools and equipment you decide to obtain; some power tools require a

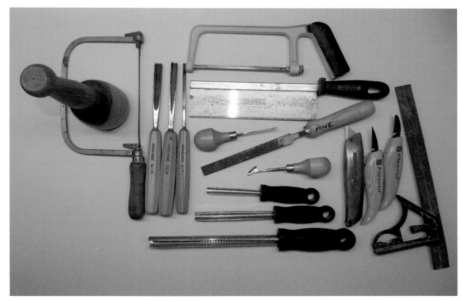

A selection of useful tools.

significant space whereas most hand and portable tools can be used in a relatively confined area.

Types of tools and equipment

Most of the tools used for stickmaking can be used for other DIY projects and hobbies, which helps to mitigate some

of the initial expense. As you progress with stickmaking, you will undoubtedly begin to collect a wider range of tools and equipment. The type of sticks you decide to make will determine the variety of tools you will require. Stick handles made from antler and horn will require tools generally designed for engineering work. A large variety of

Left: The stickmaker's workshop.

sticks can be made with a few carefully chosen tools.

The following list of tools and equipment includes a selection of those most commonly used in stickmaking.

Woodworking tools

The type of material you choose to use for making sticks and handles will determine the type and extent of tools you require. For example, if you intend to make sticks using timber alone, a range of woodworking tools as shown will get you started. As with most hobbies the range and number of tools used will generally increase and for stickmaking, this is no exception – we always seem to want another tool. Woodworking cutting tools must be kept sharp and it is important to obtain good-quality implements that will remain sharp when in use. There are various sharpening stones and rotary machines available to keep all types of tools sharp. If it is intended to carve decorations on wooden handles, small hand-held carving knives and chisels are ideal. A selection of small woodworking rasps are particularly useful for making curved surfaces on handles, as they do not clog up as much as engineering files do when used for woodwork.

Tools suitable for antler

Antler is a hard material and working antler will require a range of engineering tools such as files, rasps, hacksaws and engineering-quality drills. Most woodworking tools will not cope with antler, although the soft pith in an antler can be removed with a flat woodworking bit. If it is intended to carve antler, rotary carving machines and some suitable burrs will be beneficial; these machines can also be used to carve timber with the appropriate burrs fitted.

Tools suitable for buffalo horn

Buffalo horn is quite hard and engineering-quality tools should be used as far as possible, as woodworking tools will soon lose their edge and sharpness when used on buffalo horn. Specialist equipment is required to bend and shape buffalo horn and is described in more detail in Chapter 10, 'Equipment for Working Horn'.

Tools suitable for sheep and cow horn

Sheep and cow horn is softer than antler and buffalo horn and most good-quality tools used for working timber and antler can be used to dress sheep and cow horn. Some types of tools, such as rasps, are best suited for working with horn handles as they won't clog. Cow and sheep's horn can be successfully carved using good-quality carving knives and chisels, although rotary machines are more popular. In order to bend, bulk and shape sheep and cow horn, additional specialist equipment is required and is dealt with in Chapter 10, 'Equipment for Working Horn'. The cost and difficulty in obtaining this equipment may preclude many people from beginning this particular aspect of stickmaking, which is why it is dealt with separately.

Power tools

Air, battery or mains power tools are most useful and there are many accessories that can be used with these machines that will save time and energy. There is a vast range of power tools available. They fall into three main categories; portable, corded or fixed. Portable tools work off batteries and have the advantage that they can be used in many locations, with or without a permanent power supply. Many modern portable tools have two or more batteries

giving a longer period of use. Some tools are extremely powerful due to improving battery technology and sets of battery-operated tools are now available that operate from a single bank of batteries, which helps to keep costs down.

Corded tools require a power or air supply close to the point of use, although extension leads and air lines can be used to increase the distance from a fixed power point. Mains electric tools are generally more powerful than battery-operated versions. A disadvantage with most mains-operated equipment is that they should not be used in wet conditions unless they are designed for the purpose; it is important to have a residual current protection device that will trip and isolate the power if a fault develops in the machine or cable.

Fixed tools are static and are usually fixed to a floor or workbench, making them more stable for some activities where accuracy is important. There is a vast range of power tools available and it is very much an individual choice as to the manufacturer and type of tool to use; again try to obtain good-quality tools that have been recommended. Some typical static tools are lathes, drilling machines, planers, band and circular saws, sanders and thicknessers. Bench or floor-mounted drilling machines, sanders and band saws are probably the most popular fixed tools used by stickmakers.

Tool sets

It is not imperative to buy full sets of tools, as often only a few from the set are regularly used. Most tools can be obtained singly therefore carefully choose individual items that will definitely get used which will help keep costs to a minimum. Consider buying good quality second hand tools that are considerably cheaper than the equivalent new ones. Car boot sales or second-hand tool dealers are often worth a visit, there are some excellent bargains to be had providing you choose carefully. Occasionally when someone retires from stick-making they will sell their equipment which may be worth considering if the opportunity arises as you may find exactly what you have been looking for at a reasonable cost.

Abrasives

Abrasives are used extensively in stickmaking to shape and provide a smooth surface prior to applying a finish. There are numerous types and qualities of abrasives to choose from and they are available in many forms such as liquid, paste, paper, cloth, plastic, rolls, sheets, pads, discs and wire wool. Abrasives are designed to be used by hand or machine. Abrasives used with power tools will quickly remove material, saving time and effort, but they must be used with care as they are severe and too much material can easily and quickly be removed by these machines. Personal protective equipment (PPE) should always be worn when using any abrasive with powered machines to prevent grit and debris from causing harm or injury – it is essential to wear eye protection and suitable dust masks to avoid inhaling harmful materials. Abrasives applied by hand require more effort and are slower than using powered equipment but mistakes will be significantly reduced and your patience will often be rewarded when using this method to produce a final smooth and scratch-free surface.

Paper and cloth-backed abrasives are graded according to their 'grit'. The most aggressive grits are the lower numbers and the higher numbers are the least severe. For example 30 to 100g are coarse, 120 to 320 are medium, and

400 to 800g are fine and 1,000 and above is very fine.

Waterproof abrasive sheets commonly known as 'wet and dry' are used to provide a very smooth finish, the paper can be used dry but is best used with a drop of water that forms a fine abrasive paste which is carefully rubbed onto a surface. The paper can be obtained in a range of grits up to 2,500g, which is extremely fine. Take care when using this type of abrasive on absorbent pale-coloured surfaces as the dirt generated during the smoothing process may contaminate and discolour the material, especially light-coloured wood.

Wire wool

Wire wool is graded by a series of 0s (zeros); coarse wool is 0 rated and 0000 is the finest. Wire wool works well when it is used with a liquid or paste abrasive and will provide an excellent surface prior to applying a finish. Wire wool can also be used to apply oils, giving a lovely sheen to the surface of timbers and horn. It is used to de-nib (remove the gloss from) a finish such as varnish or lacquer so that additional coats can be applied if required. It is often used to make a smooth matt finish, which some people prefer. A word of caution; wire wool does break up during use and particles of wire can be left on the surface and will rust if exposed to wet conditions, so it is important to ensure that all particles of the wire are removed from the surface of your stick before applying a final finish.

Avoid placing any type of battery in the vicinity of wire wool as strands coming into contact with both terminals may overheat and cause a serious fire, especially in a workshop environment that may contain flammable materials. Wire wool can be mixed with vinegar to make a stain for colouring timber. Drop the wire into a glass jar containing

vinegar and leave for two or three weeks – the wire wool will slowly dissolve in the vinegar. Strain the mix into a container to remove any remnants of the wire. The mixture will darken oak and other woods; it is worth experimenting with the mixture before applying it to a finished handle or shank.

Liquid abrasives

Liquid abrasives are used to remove very fine scratches and marks; some are designed for use on vehicles and metals, however they can be used on a range of stickmaking materials such as horn, metal collars and brass ferrules. A popular black abrasive (T-Cut) designed for use on vehicles is useful for smoothing buffalo horn as the black dye is absorbed into the material, which helps to darken some of the natural markings that occur in buffalo horns. Brasso and T-Cut are regularly used for final finishing of horn handles and can be used to polish metal ferrules and collars. Avoid using liquid abrasives on timber as the dirt generated can be absorbed into the grain of the timber and will stain the surface: always test on a sample piece of material before using liquid abrasives on any absorbent material.

Files, rasps and rifflers

Files, rasps and rifflers are used for shaping most of the materials used in stickmaking.

Files

Files are generally used for engineering work on metals; they will cut most materials and are useful for working horn and antler, although the teeth may become clogged when used on some soft materials such as timber. A stiff wire brush will quickly remove most of the debris from a file. Files are graded according to their coarseness – rough and bastard cut files are the most severe, then going through second cut and down to smooth and fine. They are available in a many shapes and sizes; flat, half round, round, square and three-cornered and in a variety of lengths from 12in down to 4in in the standard ranges and are sold individually or in sets. Miniature, midget and needle sets of files are also available for very fine work.

Rasps

Rasps are similar to files but the teeth are designed to work best on softer materials such as timber, leather, horn and animal hoofs and their teeth are less likely to choke during use. Farriers use large double-sided rasps to dress horse hooves during re-shoeing and they are excellent for removing waste material from cow and sheep's horn, but are too large for finer work. It is well worth buying good-quality files and rasps, as they will retain their sharpness longer than inferior-quality ones that soon lose their edge. Millenicut rasps are designed for shaping aluminium and are excellent for using on horn; they are available in a range of shapes and sizes and have different cuts from a coarse to a smooth finish. Woodworking rasps are made especially for removing waste from timbers and using them on metal must be avoided. Traditional 'Surform' and modern stainless steel rasps 'Microplane' are used because they are very sharp and leave a reasonably smooth surface on the timber. These rasps are available in a variety of shapes and sizes and some models allow blades to be interchanged with a single handle. Japanese double-sided rasps are popular. The blade is designed not to clog up during use and they will cut most stickmaking materials such as horn, plastics and timber.

Rifflers

Rifflers are a type of rasp used to shape materials in difficult places on a carving. The end sections of rifflers are made in various shapes and profiles that enable them to reach into the most awkward positions, enabling detailed shapes to be made in tricky places. They are very useful for stickmakers who decorate handles as they will cut horn and timber and will survive for a time if used on antler. Most rifflers are double-ended and are normally sold in sets; the costs vary depending on the size and quality of the tool.

Adhesives

There are numerous types of adhesives available for general and specialist applications. Popular epoxy resins require mixing, they usually come in two equal parts and are popular with stickmakers as they provide a strong bond and can be used on most of the materials used in stickmaking; they will successfully glue timber, antler and horn and many other materials together. They are available in small or large quantities with setting times that vary from five minutes to several hours, making them very versatile for stickmaking.

Polyvinyl acetate (PVA) is an adhesive formulated principally for use with timber. It is strong and waterproof and is ideal for use with wooden sticks. Some timbers require specific adhesives because of their oil and chemical content, so when using exotic wood or some hardwoods check the suitability of the product before use.

Cyanoacrylates are commonly known as superglue and are available in a range of thicknesses and setting times from instant to several minutes. Thin superglues can be used for strengthening timber and horns as it penetrates deep into the fibre of the material, the thicker types can be used to

fill small gaps. Superglues must be used with care as some types will instantly bond skin – take precautions to ensure it does not come into contact with eyes and fingers. It is advisable to have a de-bonding solution at hand when using cyanoacrylates that can be applied in the event of an incident.

Fillers

Two-part fillers can be obtained in a few colours that are useful for setting eyes into carved birds and animal heads. The filler can also be used to fill voids and gaps as it can be smoothed with files and abrasives and then covered with paint on a decorated handle. Coloured wood fillers are available in small tubes to match different timbers and are applied directly to cracks in the timber; they can be sanded and over-painted when fully set.

Always check manufacturer's instructions because most fillers have to be used within a particular temperature range and some are very slow or may not set if the temperature is too low.

It is possible to improvise by making your own filler by using fine sanding dust and mixing it with epoxy resin to fill cracks in the same material. Another option is to drop fine sanding dust into cracks and cover it with thin superglue, which will soak into the filings and give a strong filler that can be dressed as soon as the superglue sets. Lids from empty jars and milk containers are ideal for mixing small quantities of two-part adhesives, fillers and paints; they save making a mess on your work table or bench and can be thrown away after use. Packs of lollipop sticks can be purchased from craft shops and are ideal for mixing epoxy glues. Their straight edges are also perfect for aligning handles and shanks.

Types of finishes

Always check the manufacturer's instructions before applying a finish as some may adversely react with a particular type of primer or sealer. Some finishes are applied directly to the surface while others advise using a primer or sealer prior to the application of a finish. Oils are often applied directly to the surface, especially on timber. Several types of sealers are available and they are often referred to as sanding sealers. Cellulose and acrylic sealers are popular varieties and can be applied by brush, with a cloth or aerosol spray. The sealer is applied and when it has dried, it can be rubbed down with fine abrasive making a perfect surface for a finishing product. Sealers help to raise the grain of wood which when smoothed off with a fine abrasive, makes a smoother surface in readiness for the final finishing coats. Some manufacturers advise that additional coats of sealers can be used until a satisfactory surface is achieved, while others suggest applying a single coat.

It is good practice to apply a finish to a stick as it will help to protect and preserve it for many years, and there is a huge range to choose from. Some are designed specifically for interior use only and are not suitable for outdoor applications. Suitable finishes are acrylic, cellulose, enamels, spirit- and water-based lacquers, paints and varnishes that can be obtained in gloss, satin, or matt finish depending on the individual choice, and established stickmakers all have their preferred brands and types. As mentioned it is very important when applying finishes to ensure that they are compatible with sealers or base coats – if there is any doubt try the products on a small test area first.

Always apply a finish in a dust-free, warm and dry environment to get the best results. Dust, dampness and the wrong temperature will adversely affect the finish.

Lacquer

Lacquers are generally fast setting and can be applied by brush, with a cloth or from an aerosol spray and are available in gloss, satin and matt finish. Because they are fast setting, additional coats can be applied to the surface in a short period if required. Some lacquers can be applied over paints and stains to provide protection but always ensure that the lacquer is compatible with the previous material before applying and that it is suitable for outdoor use.

Varnish

Varnishes generally take longer to dry than lacquers and should be applied in a warm, dry and clean environment. Some experienced stickmakers thin the varnish, as they prefer to use several thin coats rather than a single thick coat. When completely dry, each coat can be very lightly de-nibbed to give a key for a further coat. Several coats may be required to achieve a satisfactory finish but take care when applying it as the varnish may run if applied too thickly. If it is too thick, varnish may chip off in later use. Water- and spirit-based varnishes are available for outdoor use. When a varnish has fully dried it can be burnished to enhance the finish; burnishing paste is available although T-Cut or Brasso are often used to improve the finish.

Oil

Oils are a traditional and proven method of finishing sticks. There are several types of oils available for outdoor use and the most common used by stickmakers are linseed, Danish, teak, tung and outdoor furniture oil. Oils are popular because they soak into the timber, which helps to protect and waterproof the wood. Oil takes longer to soak into timber and dry than lacquers and varnishes, so it may take a while to apply several coats as the timber slowly absorbs the oil. When oil is completely dry it can be burnished and a pleasant-looking sheen finish can be achieved. Oils can be over-coated regularly to maintain a protective finish and are an excellent choice for a walking or working stick that is used frequently in all weathers.

Paint

Paint is rarely used as a single finish medium on walking or working sticks; it is used in small amounts to provide a coloured decoration on a carved handle or pyrography work. There are several types of paint available that are suitable for decorating sticks – model and acrylic paints are among the most popular. When the paint has fully dried always apply a compatible finish to protect painted surfaces.

Enamels

Enamels are used extensively by model makers, who only require small amounts for their work. There is a large range of colours available that can also be mixed with a compatible enamel if required, making these paints a good option for decorating handles of sticks. A separate thinner is needed to clean brushes.

Stain

Stains can improve the appearance of a shank or handle with or without bark and will often enhance knots, grains or blemishes that naturally occur in the wood. A word of warning; stains will also highlight any defects in the wood such as scratches or file marks, so ensure the surface is sound before applying. Stains are best used on untreated timber as it soaks deep into the grain, giving a long lasting colour. Most stains are spirit- or water-based and it is important to remember which type you have used so you can select a compatible protective finish that will not react with the stain. If stain is applied to dry timber it is likely to run along the grain of the wood, making it difficult to control if a fine edge is required. Also if it is intended to use a range of stains to colour a piece of timber such as a bird's head, use the lightest colours before applying dark colours; a pale-coloured stain will seldom cover a dark colour even if several coats are used. It is advisable to test stains on a similar type of timber first to ensure the result meets your requirements, as it can be difficult to obtain the correct colour and shade. Compatible stains can be mixed to provide a wide range of colours and it is advisable to keep a record of the mixing ratio used if you want to copy the colour at a later time. Stains are best used for general colouring; they are difficult to control on intricate work or carvings.

Polish

Wax polish can be used as a final finish; it will give a lovely sheen and feel to a handle or shank. Wax provides limited protection to your stick as it will wear off if a stick is used regularly in outdoor conditions. However, as with oils, it is easily over-coated and if applied regularly a beautiful finish can be maintained. Beeswax and microcrystalline polish work well when applied onto a finished surface, as do some liquid polishes used principally for vehicles and metals. Burnishing creams can be used to revive an old polish.

If you are setting up a workshop, there are a few important tools to consider. Some are listed below.

Vice

If you are setting up a workshop, a strong, fixed vice should be among your top items. Mechanics or engineering vices are strong and sturdy and are normally bolted on top of a workbench. They are used for general-purpose work and are suitable for all stickmaking jobs. Woodworking vices are usually bolted onto the side of a workbench leaving a flat worktop and are available in different sizes. Because of the position on the side of a bench, there are some limitations with their use. Swivel-headed vices are useful, especially for carving and shaping handles; some have shaped jaws that are ideal for holding shanks. Portable vices with swivel heads can be clamped onto flat surfaces such as tables and Workmates and are useful when working away from home. Handheld vices are used to hold objects safely when drilling holes – they are especially useful on powerful drilling machines that can suddenly rip an object from a hand.

Hammers and mallets

A selection of hammers is an essential part of any tool kit. The three most common types are claw hammers that can also be used to pull out nails; ball pein hammers, mainly for engineering work and useful for most jobs and cross pein hammers, ideal for driving smaller nails and pins. Most hammers are described and sold by their weight. Examples are 4oz cross pein hammers, used for delicate work; $1\frac{1}{2}$lb claw hammers, used for general joinery work and 2lb ball pein hammers, generally used for heavy engineering work. A

$1\frac{1}{2}$ lb claw or a ball pein hammer is a good choice for stickmaking.

Wooden mallets and soft-faced hammers are designed to reduce the risk of damage to all types of surfaces; they are often used in conjunction with woodworking and carving chisels to prevent the chisel handles from being damaged. A wooden mallet is a good choice for general woodwork.

Drilling machines, twist drills and bits

Hand drills are not as popular as they used to be a few years ago; battery and mains electrically-powered drills have taken over and many now incorporate screwdrivers and hammers making them extremely versatile but there are times when a hand drill or a brace and bit are useful when making a stick. Battery drills are useful tools as they can be used in remote locations and the low voltages make them safe to use outdoors in wet conditions. Bench- and floor-standing pedestal drills are a good option in a workshop if you have the space, as they can be set up to drill very accurately which is important when drilling out a stick handle.

TWIST DRILLS AND BITS
Twist drills, bits and augers are used for drilling and boring holes of different sizes in a wide variety of materials. Like most other tools, some are designed for a specific task while others can be used for general-purpose work. A set of good-quality general-purpose twist drills ranging from 1mm to 13mm will cover most stickmaking requirements; they will drill timber, horn, antler and steel. Flat spade bits are intended for cutting holes in timber and are available in a range of sizes. They are ideal for cutting the 'pith' out of antlers, ready for jointing. A blunt spade bit will tear timber, therefore always keep them sharp – they can be

purchased individually if you don't require a full set. Forstner bits are designed to cut clean, accurate holes making them a perfect choice for drilling holes into wooden handles ready for jointing; they can be obtained in sets or individually. Auger bits are designed for cutting deep, accurate holes in timber and can be used to drill the holes in shanks and handles.

Saws

Hacksaw frames will accept a range of blades that will cut most materials, especially metals and plastics. A junior hacksaw is most useful for smaller applications and will cut steel, plastics and timber; it is very handy when fitting ferrules and cutting dowel joints. Coping and fretsaws are designed for cutting shapes. They will cut a tight bend in most materials with the correct blade inserted into the frame and are particularly useful for cutting tight shapes on wood and horn handles. The thin blade performs best when used on the pull stroke, rather than pushing the blade into the material.

Hand, tenon and dovetail saws are used for accurate woodcutting. Japanese saws are becoming popular as they are good quality and are very sharp, giving clean cuts, which makes them an ideal tool for accurate joints. Some of these saws have interchangeable blades for different materials and cuts. A mitre saw is designed to cut accurate angles and is useful for cutting an angled joint or straight joint between a handle and shank. They are also used extensively for picture framing.

A folding pruning saw is ideal for cutting green shanks and branches if you intend to cut and collect your own shanks; a large, sharp pruning saw will cut through a thick branch if you want to cut your own block sticks.

Electric jig saws will cut shapes up to 2in (50mm) deep in a range of materials with the appropriate blade and are capable of cutting wooden blanks for stick handles from planked timber. If space is available, a band saw is ideal for stickmaking; it will cut tight curves in 6in (150mm) blocks of timber at various angles and with an appropriate blade fitted, it will cut most stickmaking materials. They are expensive but are a most useful tool, especially if other DIY work is undertaken in the workshop. Bench-top or floor-mounted versions are available.

Woodworking and carving chisels

There are numerous chisels made for woodworking activities and carving work. They are available individually or in sets; some are designed for use with wooden mallets and others are designed for use by hand, which are popular among stickmakers who enjoy carving small objects onto handles and shanks. It is essential that the blades are kept sharp, so a sharpening kit or stone is essential.

Carving knives

A sharp carving knife is most useful for shaping handles. Carving knives are regularly used for making decorated handles in wood and sheep's horn. Like chisels, they must be kept very sharp. Carving knives can be obtained individually or in sets with different-shaped blades for specific types of work. There is a wide range of craft knives available, some with fixed or retractable blades. These knives are very sharp and are used extensively by woodworkers and stickmakers. Most of the craft knife blades can be replaced. The Stanley knife is very popular, as it will accept various shaped blades.

Chapter 3
Ideas and Inspiration

3

Over time there have been many types and styles of sticks made; some have become classed as traditional and are generally used as working or walking sticks. There are also numerous ornately carved sticks made around the world that may relate to a country, religion or organization – many examples of these sticks can be found in specialist publications and books that are well worth investigating. Modern technology is advancing at a tremendous rate and social media sites provide a substantial amount of information on sticks that are being made within the UK and many other countries by people who are fascinated with this intriguing and compelling craft. Using books and social media sites will provide anyone with a huge amount of ideas if they wish to make either traditional or specialized sticks.

Most of this book relates to making traditional styles and is designed to help those wanting to make a range of plain or decorated sticks using timber, antler and horn. Undoubtedly the best way to learn the techniques and methods of making plain and decorated sticks is to watch, discuss, question and learn directly from an experienced stickmaker. A few professional stickmakers give lessons where complete beginners will

be taught some of the fundamental aspects of the craft and will generally make a stick to take home in one or two days. There are hundreds of excellent amateur stickmakers who are willing to show others how they make their sticks; some of these are likely to be members of a local organization or club.

Joining a stickmaking organization with likeminded members is a good way of obtaining ideas, inspiration and help. There are some incredibly clever and talented people making sticks and there will probably be a club quite close to you with several members who will be more than willing to help and give advice to any new member. Most clubs place information on the internet about themselves, with contact details for anyone wishing to enquire about membership and so on. The British Stickmakers Guild (BSG) is a national organization with hundreds of members in the UK and several overseas members. The BSG publishes a very informative quarterly magazine with input from its members; it also organizes several stick shows around the country with classes for novice and experienced stickmakers. The BSG also publishes a booklet with a list of all their members, with their addresses and telephone numbers. The

list is organized by counties and regions, which helps readers to locate other likeminded people close to their own location. Membership application forms can be obtained online or from the membership secretary of the BSG (see information at the back of the book). The BSG website also gives some information on stickmaking clubs around the UK.

Village, county and large agricultural shows around the country often host stickmaking competitions or have stickmakers on site who sell and display their sticks. These events are well worth visiting to see the types, styles and standard of sticks displayed. Most of these stickmakers are usually very keen to talk and explain their methods.

Specialist books on carving animals and birds are widely available, with detailed drawings and sketches that can be used to make a range of handles. Christmas cards, magazines, newspapers and other media often have excellent pictures of animals and birds that can be used for decorating handles and hundreds of excellent photos can be found on internet sites and downloaded for personal use. A good way to obtain your own pictures is to visit game fairs, country and agricultural shows, zoos

Left: Double woodpecker thumbstick

and farms where you can take photos of animals, poultry, game and birds of prey from several different angles so that the colouring and positions of eyes, ears, mouth and nose can be accurately reproduced on your stick handle. Modern digital cameras and mobile phones are ideal for taking photos as the images can easily and cheaply be downloaded and printed at home. Modern photocopiers are capable of increasing or reducing the size of pictures to scale, allowing a stickmaker to make an appropriately sized picture that can be transferred onto a blank by tracing the outline using carbon paper or by cutting sections of the pictures and gluing onto a blank, making it easy to mark out all the main features of the object so an accurate replica can be made.

Accurate models of popular animals and birds are very helpful as they show positions of eyes, ears, mouths, beaks, wings, legs and feet. They can be scaled up or down to suit your size and can be purchased from a wide range of shops and suppliers.

As mentioned, social media sites are rapidly expanding and more and more stickmakers and suppliers are using these sites to share information and chat about their sticks. Some stickmakers use the sites to produce guidance and advice on how they make their sticks and most are very willing to answer any questions asked. Sticks and stickmaking equipment are often available to purchase from subscribers. There are some fantastic carved handles and shanks on show, produced by some extremely talented and artistic people who have brilliant ideas that are shared across these sites. Anyone looking for ideas or inspiration should consider joining these forums as there is so much quality information available.

Stickmakers and suppliers are using websites to advertise and can be found by entering some key words into the various search engines that are accessible on smartphones and computers. Modern technology has made a tremendous amount of free information available from around the world; the amount of information is rapidly increasing and is well worth looking at to get ideas and inspiration for any new projects.

WOODPECKER THUMB-STICK FROM A SCRAP PIECE OF TIMBER

Builders, joiners, furniture makers, timber merchants and other commercial users often have surplus pieces of material left over that are usually thrown away. Stickmakers also often cut timber and other materials such as horn to make handles and again will often throw away some material with the potential to make an attractive handle, spacer, cap or even a ferrule.

My timber offcuts are thrown into bin for burning on an open fire which is used during cold spells. While collecting pieces to burn I found a piece of burr elm infested with woodworm around the outer soft wood. I had recently made a wooden thumb-stick from a small piece of timber and it occurred to me that the piece of burr could be made into an attractive and unusual thumb-stick handle. The following steps were taken to make a handle from a scrap piece destined for the fire. The burr was placed into a pan of boiling water (with some horns) to kill off any woodworm.

Step 1 An outline sketch of a pair of woodpecker heads was drawn onto the surface of the burr, the position of the eyes was marked and used as a datum point for each head.

Step 2 Two small pilot holes were drilled through the burr to use as datum points for each head. A 25mm hole was cut into the burr to form the initial opening for the thumb. The infested sections were cut from the outer edge of the burr leaving a solid section of wood to make the handle. Both head shapes were cut out of the burr using a band saw.

Step 3 Using small carving chisels and rotary burrs, both woodpecker heads and the hole for thumbs were defined.

When the head shapes were complete, the surfaces were smoothed in readiness for detailing using pyrography. The feathering detail was completed using pyrography. The handle was attached to a shank using 8mm threaded rod. The neck of the handle was carefully merged onto the shank, making a smooth transition between both handle and shank.

Step 4 The woodpecker heads were decorated using acrylic paints leaving a section of the original burr wood on the neck of the handle. A pair of glass eyes was fitted into suitably-sized eye sockets in each head. The paint was allowed to dry thoroughly before applying an acrylic finish to both the handle and shank. The finished woodpecker heads acan be seen in the photograph at the beginning of this chapter.

Looking at pictures, photos or sketches can often sow the seeds of an idea for an unusual and attractive stick handle; make a list of your ideas for future reference. Before throwing any surplus timber or horn away, carefully turn it around a few times to determine if it will make a handle for anything on your list of ideas. Several handles featured later in this book are made from small pieces of material that were too small to make a traditional handle.

Chapter 4
Collecting, Selecting and Storing Timber

There is a variety of suitable timber available for stickmaking that can be obtained by cutting and collecting your own timber from forests, woodland, parks, gardens, hedgerows and so on within the UK providing you have permission from the landowner. Some varieties of timber are more suitable for making shanks while others are better for fashioning handles – experienced stickmakers each have their preferred types and species. Occasionally an offshoot may grow from a thick branch that is large enough to make a one-piece stick, combining both a handle and shank. Some handles can also be made from contorted branches and roots; blackthorn is sometimes dug out of the ground in the hope that suitable roots will emerge to make a one-piece handle and shank. The majority of wood used for handles is planked timber and it is generally obtained from timber yards and merchants who have the facilities and equipment to cut, season, store and plank the wood.

A good, serviceable shank should to be light, strong, straight, durable and attractive. The diameter and length of shanks can vary depending on the type of stick to be made – therefore when collecting shanks, cut a range of different diameters and lengths. The typical thickness for traditional crooks and market stick shanks is between $^7/_8$in (22mm) at the tip and 1in (25mm) at the top. Short walking sticks have a smaller diameter. Most shanks will taper down to the tip; again the taper can vary from a very gentle taper to a more severe one. Full-sized crooks are best made with a light parallel shank, as a working crook is usually held about two-thirds along the shank while the crook handle is used to catch and hold a sheep. A shank with a slight taper is often accepted, as it is natural for a branch to grow with a taper. If a crook handle is too top-heavy for the shank the stick will feel heavy when used over a long period; it should feel balanced when held by the shank. Particularly tall, strong and heavy staffs may have a shank with the top diameter as much as $1^1/_4$ in (32mm) and tapering down to about 1in (25mm) at the tip. Ladies' walking sticks will be usually less than 36in (915mm) tall, a light shank with a top diameter of around 1in (25mm) reducing to around $^5/_8$in (16mm) at the bottom. When cutting and collect shanks, obtain a range of lengths and diameters from around 36in (915mm) to 60in (1,525mm) tall to cover

all requests. Remember, a long shank can be easily be cut shorter.

Timber for handles also has to be strong, durable and attractive; generally, burrs or close- grained timbers are best for making handles as they will withstand the wear and tear of a working stick better than open-grained timbers that may break or crack when in use or dropped onto a hard surface. Some popular timbers are listed below, but there are many other native and exotic timbers that can be used; it is well worth experimenting, especially when making handles. There are numerous shops, timber merchants, sawmills and DIY shops selling local and foreign timbers, giving stickmakers plenty of choice. If you intend to cut timber from woodland, parks, gardens or hedgerows remember to obtain permission from the landowner first.

The following list is a selection of timbers grown in the UK that are worth considering for making walking and working sticks. A variety of exotic foreign timbers that are suitable for making shanks and handles can be obtained from specialist timber yards and suppliers; there are too many to list in this publication.

Left: Some potential shanks.

Alder – *Alnus glutinosa*
A lightweight timber than can be used to carve handles.

Apple – *Malus*
Branches will make decent shanks; thinner branches may be too flexible.

Ash – *Fraxinus excelsior*
Ash makes sturdy shanks but the bark is uninteresting, so stickmakers will often remove the outer bark with a scraper or wire wool to reveal the more colourful inner bark, which can be enhanced by coating it with stain.

Planked ash will make good serviceable stick handles but ensure the grain is running in the correct direction, otherwise the wood may crack if dropped onto a hard floor.

Beech – *Fagus sylvatica*
Planked timbers can be used to make good handles; the branches are not the best for shanks.

Birch – *Betula pendula*
Young silver birch branches are coloured brown, turning paler when the tree matures. The bark of the tree eventually turns a silver colour and can be easily peeled from the tree. Young birch shoots make attractive shanks that are both light and strong. Mature birch makes good handles.

Blackthorn – *Prunus spinosa*
Blackthorn is regarded by many stickmakers as one of the best woods to use for shanks because of its strength, colour and knotted appearance. It is difficult and quite dangerous to cut as it is covered with sharp thorns that are poisonous, so ensure you wear appropriate protection and if your skin is punctured it is advisable to seek medical attention.

Blackthorn is used to make knob sticks and cudgels known as 'shillelaghs' in Ireland, which were originally used as throwing sticks to down small game. Shanks with regular spaced knots are the most sought after and excellent one-piece cross-handled sticks can be made by digging up a root with the shank still intact.

Blackthorn needs to be seasoned slowly in a dry, cool environment to minimize shakes (small cracks) appearing in the surface.

Box – *Buxus*
A very hard wood suitable for making carved handles or small items such as bird beaks. It is difficult to find suitable sizes for shanks. It is often used by wood turners to make finials and so on.
Broom – Sarothamnus scoparius
Plentiful timber that makes good shanks when fully seasoned.

Cherry – *Prunus avium* (Gean)
Can be used to make decent handles.
Chestnut (sweet chestnut) – Castanea
Used extensively for making National Health walking sticks. Beautiful shanks with a dark brown colour can be obtained from some of the suppliers listed.

Crab Apple – *Malus pumila/sylvestris*
A hard wood that will make good handles, and branches make attractive knobbled shanks.

Dogwood – *Cornus*
Occasionally a section with sufficient diameter may be found to make a shank.

Elm – *Ulmus procera*
Seriously affected by disease, making it more difficult to obtain. It is a good wood for carving handles if available.

Gorse – *Ulex europaeus* (furze)
A very prickly plant, making it difficult to harvest. Interesting shaped one-piece sticks can be made with the bark removed.

Hawthorn – *Crataegus monogyna*
Hawthorn makes strong, heavy shanks but the bark is quite plain in colour, so stickmakers often strip the bark from the shank and colour the wood with stain or by fuming. Like blackthorn it is covered with thorns making it difficult to cut but is not as poisonous, although the thorns can penetrate quite deeply causing severe pain, so again use appropriate protection.

Hazel – *Corylus avellana*
Hazel is the most popular wood used by stickmakers as it is light, strong, colourful, and plentiful; the shoots grow fairly straight making excellent shanks. The bark varies considerably from plain silver and brown to heavily mottled colours, so unlike some woods the attractive bark is seldom removed. Large hazel branches with a suitable offshoot are frequently used to make one-piece sticks.

Hazel (Corkscrew) – *Corylus avellana* 'Contorta'
Contorted plant, often grown in gardens. The branches will make novelty sticks and unusual-shaped handles.

Holly – *Ilex aquifolium*
Holly is a dense timber that makes heavy sticks; the bark has a tendency to wrinkle during the seasoning period so most stickmakers will strip off the bark once the shank is fully seasoned. It is recommended that the bark is left in place until the shank has fully seasoned, otherwise the shank may split. When the

bark is removed, the shank is a pale colour that can be finished beautifully, especially when the knots are left to protrude slightly. The stripped wood can be stained if a coloured finish is preferred. Holly should be given more time to season than most woods in a cool, dry place. Thick branches can be reduced in diameter, which will often reveal attractive patterns.

Honeysuckle – *Lonicera percynemum*
Honeysuckle is climbing plant that wraps itself tightly in a clockwise spiral around young trees and their branches, forming deep grooves in the host plant as it grows. The result is a 'twisty' shank, much sought after by stickmakers and their customers.

Hornbeam – *Carpinus betulus*
When available, the timber is suitable for carving handles and smaller branches will make a decent shank.

Ivy – *Hedera helix*
A common climbing plant that grows on walls, buildings and trees. It can be used to make unusual one-piece shaped walking sticks, providing it is allowed to fully season.

Laburnum – *Laburnum anagyroides*
This popular wood is often used by turners and carvers because of its distinctive colouring. The wood will make interesting handles, especially when turned into round knob stick handles.

Lime – *Tilia* sp.
The common wood is used extensively by wood carvers as it is light, strong and close-grained, making it an ideal timber for carving decorated stick handles.

London Plane – *Platanus*
Planked timber will make an excellent handle, with an attractive grain pattern running through the timber.

Oak – *Quercus robur*
The wood is heavy, hard and dense. Handles can be made from oak but are likely to be on the heavy side. Turned shanks can be made and stained to make sturdy walking sticks.

Poplar – *Populus*
A popular timber used by wood turners, planked timber will make nice handles.

Rhododendron – *Rhododendron ponticum*
An abundant wide-spread evergreen plant. Excellent naturally shaped and strong handles can be found from the branches, although it is difficult to find suitable lengths to make decent shanks.

Rowan – *Sorbus aucuparia* (often called Mountain Ash)
The timber is sometimes used to make one-piece sticks. It is suitable for carving handles.

Sycamore – *Acer pseudoplatanus*
Can be used successfully to make handles.

Sweet Chestnut – *Castanea*
Makes excellent and attractive shanks with a dark bark.

Walnut – *Juglans regia*
Will make excellent handles, but not the best timber for shanks.

Yew – *Taxus baccata*
The heartwood has beautiful colouring, which can be used to make handsome handles. Quality shanks can be made from branches but are difficult to obtain.

Cutting, collecting and storing timber

Some stickmakers prefer to cut their own timber for handles and shanks from hedgerows, gardens, coppices and woodland when the sap is at its lowest, which in deciduous trees is during the winter. Shanks from evergreen trees are usually cut after they have fruited, again when the sap is reputed to be at its lowest. However, experienced stickmakers will cut a stick when they find it because if it is left it can be difficult to find again or – even worse – someone else may find it and take it home. Timber can be cut at any time of the year providing it is given sufficient time to dry out and season thoroughly in a dry, cool environment. Timbers are best treated with a sealant to prevent them from drying out too fast, which can cause the timber to split and crack. Some old paint or varnish applied to the end of shanks or blocks will help to prevent the wood from drying out too quickly; however, if you intend to season a lot of timber it will be worth obtaining a bona fide sealant from a reputable supplier. Another option is wrapping the timber with polythene or cling film, creating a mini climate within and slowing the speed at which timber dries, reducing the risk of it cracking. This method apparently works well with small handle-size pieces of timber and the block section on one-piece sticks.

Always cut shanks longer and slightly thicker than required for your finished stick as the diameter of the wood will shrink slightly as it dries and shakes (small cracks) may appear in the ends of the wood if it is dried too quickly. Do not cut offshoots or thorns too close to the unseasoned shank, as shakes may appear in the shank as the stick dries. They are best removed when the wood has fully seasoned.

The tools required to cut shanks are; a

Equipment for cutting shanks.

folding pruning saw or a bow saw to cut branches, a pair of secateurs to cut offshoots, a pair of gloves to protect your hands and a ball of string or a couple of leather straps (dog collars are good) to tie your sticks in a bundle to make them easier to carry back to your vehicle. Pruning loppers can also be used to cut shank-sized timber. When cutting blackthorn or hawthorn it is advisable to wear eye protection and heavy clothing as the thorns can cause a serious injury, especially blackthorn, which is toxic.

Block sticks can be cut using a pruning saw but it is difficult and laborious; a sharp bow saw or a coarse-bladed rip saw is better. The ideal tool is a chainsaw, providing the user is competent with its use. The problems with cutting block sticks is that a large section of a tree is cut down to obtain a large enough block for a handle such as a shepherd's crook; the next problem is carrying heavy blocks and tools back to a vehicle. The final consideration is that a lot of waste timber is left behind. It is important that you have permission from the landowner to cut such large sections of trees down. The ideal solution is to persuade a coppice worker to cut block sticks on your behalf when it is time to coppice sections of woodland. It is best if you are in attendance to identify and advise on where to cut the block if this is permissible; you can also help to clear up the debris.

When a stick has fully seasoned, it can be made into a shank; the length can be reduced and the knots cut closer. Shanks of 1in (25mm) or less in diameter will season in about twelve months but it is recommended to let them thoroughly dry out for two or more years before use. It is advisable to protect all timbers against woodworm and boring insects by dipping, spraying or wiping the wood with a woodworm killer solution. It is recommended that shanks are treated at least annually to prevent infestation, although some products are supposed to prevent infestation for several years. The life cycle of these pests is three to four years; the tiny beetle lays her eggs in small cracks and crevices, generally in springtime, the eggs hatch and the minute grub eats and burrows its way into the timber and grows in size. The grub may stay inside the timber for several years before emerging, leaving a tell-tale hole. During this time, the grub will have eaten its way along a substantial section of the timber. If several eggs were laid it is probable that numerous grubs will be active in the timber, quickly rendering it useless. When the grubs emerge they hatch into beetles, they mate with other beetles and the whole process begins again. There is no way of telling if the tiny grub has entered the wood until it emerges several years later. Grubs may be present in the wood before it is cut or used, which is why woodworm holes sometimes appear long after a stick has been finished and varnished – especially if it has missed being treated with a woodwork killer during storage. This is why an annual treatment is recommended on raw shanks.

Store shanks in order of the year they were cut and use the oldest first, allowing sufficient time for them to season. Shanks can be stored upright in racks or bundles or horizontally in bundles in the apex section of your garage or shed roof, making sure that there is sufficient space to allow fresh air to circulate around them to aid the drying process.

It is well worth taking sticks out of storage once a year to examine them and discard any that are unsuitable. Take the opportunity to cut the remaining sticks to some set lengths of your choice; examples are 40in (1,200mm), 55in (1,400mm) and 60in (1,530mm) to make storage more orderly. Also take this opportunity to roughly straighten the shanks using a steam box to heat the sticks. This annual exercise has several advantages. It gets rid of any unsuitable sticks, the sticks are cut into manageable lengths, making storage simpler when selecting shanks from your store; and finally, heating the complete stick in the steam box will destroy any bugs that are present in the wood. Treat all the sticks with woodworm killer before restacking them in their year order; the combination of heat and chemical treatment should keep your shanks free from infestation.

If you are unable to cut and collect your own shanks, a large variety is available from several of the suppliers listed at the back of the book. They can be obtained in their natural condition or straightened, with or without bark. Some are stripped and stained in a range of colours; others are available with a carved spiral pattern. Some suppliers do not deliver shanks to your home – they have to be collected from the supplier's premises.

Shank store.

Shanks for sale.

Chapter 5
Straightening Shanks

When your sticks have fully seasoned they can be straightened; green unseasoned sticks will always try to revert back to their original shape. Allow a 1in (25mm) diameter stick to season for a minimum of twelve months and preferably longer before attempting to straighten or dress it. Allow larger diameter shanks and block sticks to season for longer periods. It will take some time to build up a stock of seasoned shanks so in the interim period, while the cut sticks are seasoning, it is advisable to obtain seasoned shanks from suppliers or other stickmakers. It is not recommended to use unseasoned timber to make handles or shanks.

To straighten a bent stick, it has to be heated in order to remove the bends and straighten the timber. Wet or dry heat can be used when straightening or bending.

There are various ways of using wet heat: timber can be submersed in boiling water or in hot, wet sand in order to heat it in readiness for bending, but this is impractical for shanks in a small workshop environment. A popular method of straightening sticks is to use steam as the heat medium; sticks held over or in a source of steam will heat up to soften the timber sufficiently to

remove any bends. A shank held over the spout of a boiling kettle or the top of an open pan or urn will heat up enough to remove bends. Placing sacks or rags over a boiling urn will heat up the rags; sticks are placed in the hot rags until they are soft enough to remove any bends. The preferred method of using steam is to make a steam box or tube that will hold several shanks at a time. A wallpaper-stripping steam heater is used to boil a quantity of water, the steam is fed into the base of the steam box or tube and all the sticks are heated simultaneously. The shanks will be hot enough to straighten after about ten minutes in the steam. The hot stick is straightened using a simple wooden jig to remove the bends; the process is explained below. This is an excellent method of removing the worst bends from sticks as several sticks can be quickly straightened in a short time and is an ideal way of preparing seasoned sticks for storage, as any wood-boring insects will be destroyed and there is no risk of scorching or burning the timber. When it is time to take a stick for use as a shank it may require 'fine tuning' to make it perfectly straight; this can be done using dry heat.

Dry heat is achieved using an electric

hot air gun that is normally used for removing and stripping paints and varnish. A gas torch is an option but this method is seldom used as naked flames can scorch the timber and there is a risk of causing a fire in a workshop full of combustible materials.

Heat from the hot air gun is carefully applied along the bent section of the stick until it heats up sufficiently to remove the bend. The bent section of the stick can be gently forced in the opposite direction of the bend in a jig or over your knee until it straightens; the straightened section is held in place a short time until it sets into its new position. If there are several bends to straighten along the stick, these are heated and straightened in sequence using the same technique. Is advisable to begin the process at one end of the stick and progress along to the other end in sequence until it is straight along its length. It may take more than one session to get a perfectly straight stick. Straightening blocks and boards can be made quite easily from discarded pieces of timber with a few woodworking tools. A pair of wooden straightening blocks designed to work in a bench vice can quickly be cut out of a piece of 4in x 4in square timber around 6in in length on a

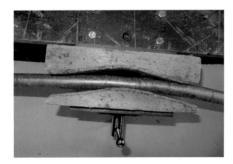

Straightening blocks and vice.

band saw. Smaller blocks can be made using 2in x 2in timber and cut out with a jig or coping saw. Pre-made pairs of blocks can be obtained from some of the suppliers listed.

A simple straightening board can be made using offcuts of plywood or planked timber. Select a piece of planked timber or plywood about 8in wide x 1in thick and around 18in long. Fix a piece of 2in x 2in square timber underneath the board which is used to clamp the board into a vice or Workmate. Cut a pair of half round blocks from a piece of $1^{1}/_{2}$in planked timber and bolt these onto the board, leaving sufficient space for the thickest stick to fit between the pair of blocks. Ensure the timber sections are bolted and glued firmly onto the board as a substantial amount of pressure is applied when removing stubborn bends. A few holes can be drilled in the board to hold the shank in position with wooden pegs until it cools during the straightening process. The same technique and jigs are used on sticks heated with wet and dry heat.

Two types of simple steam containers can be made; the first method uses a section of round, thick-walled plastic pipe about 4in to 6in in diameter. The second method involves making a timber or plywood box of sufficient length, depth and width to contain a few

sticks. The dimensions are not critical as long as they will hold a few bent sticks. If the sticks are too long for the containers they can be turned around after one end has been straightened.

The steam pipe version is very simple to make. Obtain a piece of thick-walled 4in to 6in diameter pipe about 50in long. Drill a hole (about 1in or 25mm) in the bottom of the pipe that is large enough to fit the hose from the wallpaper steamer into. Fasten the pipe to a square base-board about 18″ square, using a pair of shelving brackets so the pipe is in an upright position which will allow the steam to rise up through the sticks. Leave the top of the pipe open for the steam to escape. The simple container shown in the illustration is made from a piece of 4in diameter plastic pipe with a thick wall. Once the pipe is attached to a base board a hole is cut into the bottom to enable the hose of a wallpaper-stripping machine to be inserted. The hole also allows surplus water to drain away from the container when in use. The container in the illustration will hold between six and eight shanks at a time, which is an advantage if you want to straighten several in a session. The one disadvantage with this piece of pipe is that it is too short to hold a long shank, so they are turned around after one end has been straightened.

A wooden container can be made from planks of timber or plywood with sufficient thickness to prevent them from

Steam pipe.

warping. A hinged lid is a good option so access to replenish or remove sticks is simple. The wooden container can be used in an upright or tilted position, providing it allows the steam to rise through the sticks.

Do not seal the containers; allow the steam to vent freely into the atmosphere. Custom and practice imply that when a stick has been seasoned, straightened and cut to length and is ready for use, it generally becomes known as a shank.

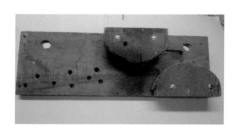

Simple straightening board.

A SHORT GUIDE TO STRAIGHTENING STICKS

Step 1. Heat a bent stick and place the middle of a bend between a pair of blocks fixed onto a straightening board. A vice with blocks inserted is another option.

Step 2. Reverse the bend by pulling it against one of the blocks until it straightens, hold it for a moment in position until the shank cools and sets. Pegs can be used to hold the shank in place. While the shank is warm, it can be slightly adjusted. Reheat and reposition to remove any further bends. Using the vice, tighten the blocks and force the bend out of the stick so it goes slightly beyond the parallel (in other words reversing the bend), leave for a few moments until the stick cools.

Slowly release the pressure on the blocks and observe how much the stick has straightened. Retighten or slacken off the blocks depending on the position of the stick while it is warm. Release the stick when it has cooled.

Step 3. Repeat the process along the stick until all the bends have been straightened. It may take a few attempts to obtain a perfectly straight shank. The stick can be reheated if the bend is very stubborn and requires further straightening. Dog legs and other severe bends can sometimes be removed using a jig designed for removing these stubborn curves. The jig featured will remove a severe bend and hold the heated stick in place until it has cooled.

The art of straightening shanks will quickly improve with experience; begin with sticks that have gentle curves or bends and you will soon begin to 'feel' the wood move.

Pre-straightened shanks

If you do not have the equipment or facilities to cut and straighten your own sticks, fully seasoned and straightened shanks that are ready for use can be obtained from some of the suppliers listed. These prepared shanks are ideal for beginners and experienced stickmakers who have not had the chance to forage in woods and hedgerows to cut and collect their own. By using these shanks initially, it allows you time to collect, season and straighten your own. Some of the suppliers carry several types of wood and different sizes of shanks that would make excellent walking or working sticks.

Stick in straightening board.

Bend being reversed.

Straightening jig for severe bends.

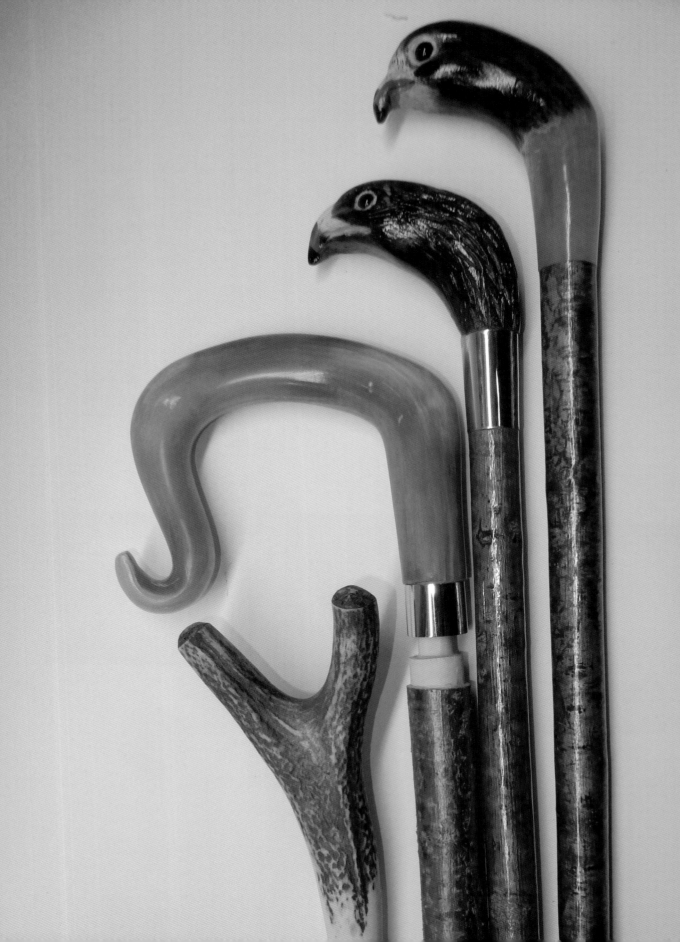

Chapter 6
Jointing

The most important component of any stick is the joint. Joints are used to fix handles and ferrules onto shanks and in some instances decorations to handles and shanks. Even a one-piece stick requires a joint to fasten a ferrule onto the tip to prevent the shank from wearing. It is crucial to make strong and reliable joints that look neat and attractive and will withstand all the wear and tear that a walking or working stick will be subjected to during its lifetime. A high percentage of problems with walking and working sticks occur because badly made joints fail. These failures are disappointing for the owner and with a little care and attention can be avoided. Too often joints fail because the maker has not given sufficient thought to bonding and fitting the various parts of sticks together. A badly made joint spoils the appearance of a stick, as well as demonstrating an inadequate level of care in making it.

A joint between a shank and handle must be strong enough to hold the handle in position and be capable of coping with the stress of a person or animal leaning, pulling and twisting the stick, which imparts a considerable amount of force on the joint. The joint must last for the working life of a stick that will be used in all types of weather and conditions, so it is essential that the joints are well made and glued together using top-quality adhesives suitable for outdoor use in all conditions and environments. When making a working stick or crook consider making an angled joint between the handle and shank, because these joints help to prevent the handle from twisting if the stick is subjected to excessive force or stress (for example when catching sheep). An angled joint looks best when it is angled up towards the nose of the handle. Using an angled joint slightly increases the surface area between the handle and shank and helps to increase the strength of the joint. Three joints with angles of five, ten and fifteen degrees are shown later to give the reader an idea of which angle joint to make. Angled joints can be made between any handle material and shank.

Jointing ferrules

The most popular ferrules used were made from brass with a steel tip but unfortunately they are no longer in production. The best modern alternative brass ferrules are made with a heavy brass tip that will withstand extensive wear and tear. A cheaper model with a thinner brass tip is available, but they do not last as long as the heavier model. Untipped ferrules can be made from various other metal tubes such as copper, brass and stainless steel; they will reduce wear and tear but will absorb water into the base of the shank unless it is sealed or a tip is fitted. Horn, acrylic and hard-wood tips can be made to protect the shank and are fitted using threaded rod or a steel pin. The ferrule is dressed down to match with the diameter of the shank; these ferrules can be made longer than a standard brass ferrule to make a slightly longer shank if required.

Left: Sicks with a range of joints.

GUIDE TO JOINTING BRASS FERRULES

Step 1. Select an appropriately sized ferrule to suit the diameter of the shank. Using a junior hacksaw, cut a shallow circle around the shank that matches the depth and thickness of the ferrule.

Step 2. Use a sharp knife to cut surplus wood away from the ring towards the bottom of the stick in the shape of the ferrule (some ferrules are parallel, others are tapered), until the ferrule almost pushes onto the new dowel.

Step 3. Use the sharp knife to carefully cut back from the tip to the ring to form a sharp edge on the shoulder for the ferrule to fit against. Keep testing the fit of the ferrule and when the ferrule is close to fitting, use a strip of abrasive cloth to smooth and round off the surface so a tight fit is achieved between the ferrule and shank.

Step 4. Use a good-quality epoxy or other strong adhesive and smear it on the base of the tip and around the circumference of the shank. Fit the ferrule and turn it around so the adhesive spreads within the ferrule. Gently tap the ferrule in place so it butts up against the shoulder. Wipe away any surplus glue and allow the joint to set. Smearing adhesive on the base of the tip helps to seal the wood against water ingress.

Alpine spikes

Cross-country and hill walkers regularly walk over rough terrain and will often request that an alpine spike is fitted onto their favourite hiking stick. Alpine spikes are fitted in the same way as metal ferrules; cut a ring, cut away surplus wood and make a sharp-edged shoulder to butt the spike against. The main

Cut a ring around shank.

Removing surplus wood.

Check the fit of the ferrule.

Complete fitting the ferrule.

difference is that they have a much longer taper designed to give them more strength for the arduous conditions they are used for and generally there is a small hole in the spike, allowing it to be pinned onto the shank, improving its strength and reliability. Because the stick will be used in all weather and ground conditions use a good-quality adhesive to smear all of the tip of the shank and the inside of the spike to make a strong and waterproof joint. Finish by inserting a rust-proof pin or screw through the hole into the ferrule tip.

A fitted alpine spike.

Bone, horn, acrylic or timber ferrules

Ferrules can be made from a variety of materials but, unlike commercially made ferrules and spikes, they are usually hand-made to fit a specific shank. Most metal ferrules and spikes are hollow and are joined by making a dowel on the tip of the shank. Solid turned buffalo horn, metals, acrylics and timber are available in different sizes that will make strong and hard-wearing ferrules. The turned material is joined onto the shank with a simple butt joint. The base of the shank and the turned ferrule are both cut

A buffalo horn ferrule.

perfectly flat and are joined by drilling an appropriate-sized hole in each. A short piece of brass or stainless steel rod (to prevent rust) is used to form the joint, which is glued together using good-quality adhesive. When the adhesive has set, the new ferrule is dressed so it fits and blends perfectly with the tip of the shank.

Rubber ferrules

A considerable number of people will request that a rubber ferrule is fitted onto a stick because they do not slip on smooth surfaces in the same way that a standard ferrule does. Older people feel more confident with a rubber ferrule and are not as concerned about the appearance of a stick as perhaps a younger person or collector may be. A huge range of rubber ferrules is available. Some are made to fit on furniture legs; others are made to fit on NHS walking aids and similar appliances. Ferrules specifically designed for walking and working sticks are more substantial, with strong walls and a thick, non-slip base. The most substantial of these are also fitted with a steel washer inside, giving them more strength and longer wear and are a good choice to use on all your sticks. Rubber ferrules can be simply pushed onto the shank providing they are a tight fit; however it is recommended that they are glued in position with a waterproof

A selection of rubber ferrules.

adhesive. Rubber ferrules work successfully when slipped over metal ferrules and are a popular option to offer customers and users, as the stick is well protected against wear and tear and the rubber ferrules are easily changed.

Commonly used joints

Four methods are frequently used to join handles and shanks together.

1. A home-made wooden dowel cut onto a shank and inserted into a handle.
2. A turned wooden dowel is inserted in the handle and shank.
3. A threaded steel rod is inserted in the handle and shank.
4. Brass connectors or threaded inserts are used to make take-apart joints.

The first three joints are permanent, take-apart joints allow sticks to be dismantled and are useful for travellers and users who wish to change handles or dismantle a stick to reduce its length.

MAKING A DOWEL JOINT

A dowel is a simple wooden peg that is carefully cut onto a shank that fits into a suitably sized hole drilled into the handle; the dowel is then glued into the handle. Dowel sizes vary depending on the size and type of handle used but will generally be in the range of 12mm to 18mm in diameter and around $2^1/_2$ in (65mm) long. A precisely made dowel joint is the preferred joint of many stickmakers as it is simple, light and strong and does not influence the balance of a stick as much as a threaded metal rod.

Step 1. Drill an appropriately sized hole into the centre of your chosen handle approximately $2^1/_2$ in (65mm) deep. The diameter of the hole will depend on the size of the handle but will generally be between $^1/_2$ in (12mm) and $^5/_8$ in (16mm). The peg is made to be a tight push fit into this hole.

Step 2. Using a junior hacksaw, cut a clean shoulder around the shank about 2 in (65mm) from the top. Note the length of pegs can vary.

Step 3. Use a sharp knife to cut away surplus timber and begin shaping the peg. A rasp can also be used to remove the surplus material if preferred. Keep checking the peg against the hole in the handle, stop cutting away material as it approaches the correct diameter and make a parallel peg with a clean edge against the shoulder of the shank.

Step 4. Use a strip of cloth abrasive about 80 to 100 grit to finish and round off the peg until it fits neatly into the handle. Check that the handle and shank are aligned; make any adjustments necessary to maintain alignment between the handle and shank.

Step 5. Mark the position that makes the

Drill a hole into the handle.

Ring cut onto shank.

Surplus material being removed.

Peg rounded.

Mark the position of the best fit.

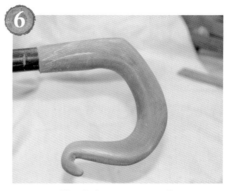

Check the joint is good.

Maintain pressure on the joint.

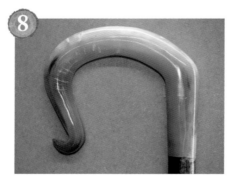

Make a neat, close joint.

best joint between the handle and shank using masking tape. Draw a pencil line along both the handle and shank when the best fit is achieved.

Step 6. Before applying an adhesive, carry out a final check to ensure the peg is a tight fit and the handle butts up to the shoulder all around, making a close-fitting joint between the handle and shank. Check that the handle and shank are aligned.

Step 7. Glue the shank and handle together with a good-quality adhesive and maintain pressure on the joint until the adhesive has fully set. Wipe off any surplus adhesive that has been squeezed from the joint before it sets.

Step 8. When the adhesive has set, begin to merge the handle and shank together ensuring that a neat, close-fitting joint is achieved between the two components.

TURNED WOODEN PEG JOINT

Turned dowelling can be purchased from most DIY stores and timber merchants and it is available in a variety of timbers and several diameters, giving plenty of options. The dimensions used in turned dowels are the same as those used in home-made peg joints. The diameter of the dowel is governed by the size of hole drilled into the handle. The same size hole is also drilled into the shank. A flat or an angled joint can easily be made using turned dowelling.

Step 1. Cut a flat or an angle on both the handle and shank. Angled joints can be cut using a saw or a sanding machine with a table and mitre fence attachment.

Step 2. Drill an appropriate sized hole in the centre of both the shank and handle, each hole to a depth of around $2^1/_2$ in (65mm), ensuring that both holes will align the shank and handle.

Step 3. Cut a suitable length of turned dowel that is the same diameter as the two holes, slightly round off both ends of the dowel to reduce the 'piston effect' that a flat surface may cause. The dowel may need sanding down slightly so that it fits into the holes in the shank and handle.

Turned dowelling.

Step 4. Assemble the joint before applying any adhesive, to check that the joint is a perfect fit and the handle and shank are aligned. Make any necessary adjustments and ensure the joint surfaces are close fitting.

Step 5. Apply a suitable adhesive to all the surfaces and assemble the joint, ensuring that it is kept under pressure until the adhesive has fully set. Wipe off any adhesive that has been squeezed from the joint.

Steel peg joint using threaded rod

The steps taken to make a joint using threaded rod are basically the same as making a wooden peg joint. Steel or other metals and materials can be used instead of using wood in peg joints. Aluminium, brass, stainless steel, carbon fibre, nails or round steel are all options that can be used. Most stickmakers choose to use steel threaded rod from the above options; it is a tried and tested method, chiefly because it makes a strong and secure joint. The threaded surface helps to make a strong bond in the handle and shank and also reduces the piston effect that can occur when using a tight-fitting round bar. The two most popular sizes used are 6mm and 8mm diameter, anything larger will make the joint too heavy and lighter rod will not be strong enough. Some traditional stickmakers do not use threaded rod in sticks, especially when making shepherd's crooks using sheep or cow horns. Some failures have occurred in working crooks with threaded rod joints, possibly caused by frequently tapping the stick on the ground, which causes the shank to split. Wooden peg joints have proved to be more reliable in working crooks. If you

are requested to make a shepherd's crook, ask the new owner which type of joint is preferred. Also when selling a crook, advise the new owner which type of joint was used.

Take-apart joints

Occasionally someone requires a stick that can be dismantled. Sticks can be transported more easily when travelling by air, coach, sea or car if they can be dismantled and placed within luggage or some form of container. A few owners also like to change the handles or shorten and extend the length of a shank. Plain or flanged connectors and threaded inserts allow stick components to be dismantled.

Using brass connectors

Plain or flanged brass connectors can be used to make joints between handles and shanks and between sections of a shank. The flanged joint is 1in (25mm) in diameter, both connectors use $^5/_{16}$in (8mm) threads. The flanged connector provides a pair of true surfaces that pull together making a strong and accurate joint, whereas the plain connector relies on the surfaces of the stick material to make the accurate joint. Both types of connectors have to be carefully and accurately fitted into the stick components so the two sections are perfectly aligned, especially if two sections of a shank are to be joined; any misalignment will be noticeable and will spoil the whole appearance of the stick.

JOINTING A SHANK WITH A FLANGED CONNECTOR

Step 1. Select a straightened and fully seasoned shank that will not move during use. Locate a point in the shank that is exactly 1in (25mm) in diameter, mark the point and cut the shank in two. If a smaller diameter shank is used, any excess brass will have to be carefully removed from the two flanges using files and abrasives to reduce the size of the flanges to match the diameter of the shank.

Step 2. Drill holes into each section of the shank of a diameter and depth to suit the outside diameter of the brass connector, ensuring that both holes are exactly in the centre and are aligned with the shank.

Step 3. Dry assemble the two sections of the shanks with the flanged connector tightened together to check the alignment of the shank is accurate. If it is not perfectly straight, enlarge the holes using a drill 0.5mm larger than the original size. This will (hopefully) allow sufficient movement of the shanks on the tightened flanges to achieve a straight joint. Carefully check before gluing the joint.

Step 4. Use a straight-edged surface such as a plank of timber or piece of angle iron to clamp both sections of the connector and shank together, ensuring that all the components are perfectly in alignment; use a slow-setting adhesive to glue the parts together. A slow-setting adhesive will allow a little time to make any final adjustments. Allow the adhesive to fully set before releasing and removing the clamps.

Step 5. The shank can be uncoupled and when reassembled, it will join together in the same position time after

Flanged connectors used for jointing.

Flanged connector fitted into shank.

Both brass connectors fitted in shank.

A straight edge used to hold shank in position.

time. When satisfied that the joint is good, fit a handle and a ferrule.

Using threaded inserts

Threaded inserts are commonly used to join a handle onto a shank. The most popular method is to fit an insert into a shank and glue a section of threaded rod into the handle.

Inserts generally come in two sizes, 6mm and 8mm. They require a larger hole to be drilled into the shank, for example a 6mm insert will require an 8mm hole to be drilled. The insert is glued and then screwed into the hole using an Allen key. Handles with threaded rods can be interchanged giving the user lots of options. There are two types of inserts, plain and flanged. The plain flange can be sunk deeper into the hole so the joint pulls against the surface of the shank while a flanged

A pair of threaded inserts.

Threaded insert fitted into shank.

insert remains on the surface. A length of threaded rod to match the thread of the insert is fitted and glued into the handle, leaving a short length protruding to screw into the insert. It is important that both the insert and threaded rod are positioned so the handle and shank are perfectly aligned and the joint is a tight fit with no gaps evident before gluing. A rolled collar is often used when making take-apart joints, as the handle will enter the collar making a more attractive and secure joint.

Fitting a collar

Sometimes a collar is fitted to form an integral part of the joint. Collars will add strength to a joint, which can be beneficial for sticks that will be subjected to arduous work and conditions. They also enhance the appearance of sticks; brass, copper, nickel and silver collars are often engraved with the initials of the owner or an emblem of some kind. Collars are made from various materials including brass, copper, stainless steel, horn, antler and timber and there are various shapes to choose from. The worst method of fitting a collar is to slide it up a shank and over the joint between the handle and shank. Rarely does a collar fit correctly when using this method. A plain collar has to be fitted exactly if it is to enhance the appearance of the stick, but there is a slight amount of leeway when fitting a rolled collar as the shank or handle can enter into the collar. Rolled collars work well when interchangeable handles are used; the collar is fitted tightly onto the shank and is a permanent fixture, the interchangeable handles are made so that they enter into the rolled collar making a tight-fitting and strong joint.

Joints on decorations

Occasionally small, fragile decorative items need to be joined onto a section of a stick or handle. Stickmakers will often replace a vulnerable piece such as an ear or a beak with a separate piece of stronger material such as horn or antler to improve the strength of the original material. There are several two-part putty-like substances available that can be kneaded together that will make a strong piece for a decoration. These delicate items have to be very carefully joined and often, small pins are used to improve the strength of the joint. It is important that a tight joint is made between the two materials in order to conceal it before the decoration is completed. Extreme care is required when making sure the surfaces to be joined are a perfect fit; fine tools and patience are needed to achieve such precision. Superglues are regularly used to fix small items as they are extremely strong and quick setting. They are now being used in conjunction with baking powder to strengthen vulnerable parts. Baking powder is used to cover the part, which is then coated with superglue; the two react and make a hard surface that can be dressed.

It cannot be emphasized sufficiently; joints are the most important part of a stick. They must be made with care and attention in order for them to be strong, reliable and unobtrusive.

Chapter 7
Making One-Piece Sticks

A one-piece stick is made from a single piece of timber that has been cut from a tree or shrub. Making one-piece sticks can be simple or difficult. Some of the simplest, most functional and reliable one-piece sticks can be made with a few basic tools. Others are difficult to collect, take a long time to season and are difficult to make. Examples of both categories are included in this chapter.

Should you decide to cut and collect your own timber, selecting a suitable section that will make a one-piece stick is quite challenging – remember you must allow it to fully season before use. The heavier the timber, the longer it needs to season; it is commonly accepted that a 1in (25mm) thick piece of timber needs to season for a year, so it follows that a section 4in (100mm) thick or a section of 6in (150mm) thickness will require a much longer time to season. It is not strictly linear but allow sufficient time for a block to fully season. Many styles of sticks can be made from a single piece of timber – imagination is the key, picturing in your mind's eye what type of stick can be made from a piece of a particular shape. Some of the

A pair of natural thumb sticks.

Seasoned block sticks.

suppliers listed at the end of the book sell seasoned timber suitable for making a variety of one-piece sticks, if you want to begin making quickly rather than wait for your own cut wood to season.

The most common one-piece sticks are the walking sticks made from chestnut for the NHS and they are the only walking sticks made to comply with a British Standard. These have been heated using wet heat and generally have all the bark stripped from them; the rounded handles are shaped and tied in position while the shank is still hot, and

the shanks are quickly straightened using the same heat. It only takes the experienced makers a few minutes to shape and straighten these walking sticks. Some are stained while others remain their natural colour; their height and weight vary to accommodate the hundreds of users. Most are fitted with rubber ferrules to prevent them from slipping on pavements and other hard surfaces; the sticks are sturdily made providing safe support for their users. They often end up for sale in charity shops for a small amount of money.

Left: A selection of one-piece sticks. Photo by Colin Mills.

Making simple one-piece sticks

Very simple, functional and reliable walking and working sticks can be made with a few basic tools, allowing people of all ages and ability to have a go at making themselves or a friend a really useful and usable stick that will last a long time with a little care and attention. Some examples of simple one-piece sticks that can easily be made are; a hiking staff, a thumb stick, a cross-head stick and a knob stick. Cut from local woodland using a small garden pruning saw (a pair of loppers could be used) and allow them to season in a cool, dry wood store. During the storage period, all the shanks should be treated to reduce the risk of infestation from woodworm. By carefully selecting shanks and using their natural shapes, practical and serviceable sticks can be made without having to make any substantial changes and they will last for many years with a little regular care. The following tools can be used to make

these; a vice, a junior hacksaw, a flat rasp, a round rasp, and a couple of pieces of 120 grit and 180 grit abrasives. Raw linseed oil was used to finish the sticks and can be regularly over-coated to protect and preserve the timber. A bench vice was used to hold the sticks, but a clamp-on vice could be used.

A hiking staff

The first stick is a hiking staff. This is simply a long natural shank that has grown in a fairly straight direction. The top of the staff is rounded off with a rasp, followed by using abrasives to make the top smooth and more comfortable to hold. The whole length of the staff is rubbed down to smooth off the bark and to remove any protrusions caused by small twigs or branches with a 180 grit abrasive. A rubber ferrule can be fitted over the base and glued in position.

Protect the stick with a few coats of raw linseed oil. An elasticated lanyard can be slipped over the staff to give the user the

option of extra support if required. Once the timber has seasoned, a hiking staff can be made within a short period of time.

Natural thumb sticks

Natural thumb sticks can be found growing in several species of trees. A pair of branches grow outwardly from a main stem to form a 'V' or 'U' shape that can be used as a thumb stick, providing the size of the stick and the 'V' or 'U' shape is suitable. It can take quite some time to locate a really well-shaped thumb stick in a large wood. Natural thumb sticks are usually thicker at the bottom of the shank because of the way the branch grows from the mother tree to the 'V' shape at the top, which is the thinnest section. When looking for a natural thumb stick, avoid cutting a shank where the lowest end is considerably larger and heavier than the top as it will make the stick unbalanced and awkward to use; try to find a fairly parallel shank that will improve the balance and feel of the stick.

A typical shank on a thumb stick will be about 1in (25mm) diameter. It is important that the 'V' is wide enough in the base to allow a thumb to fit comfortably between the legs. If the legs have sufficient thickness, their shape can be altered using a rasp to open them up a little, making the stick more usable.

Smooth the surface bark off using an 180 grit abrasive. Again, a rubber ferrule can be slipped over the tip and the whole stick treated with oil for protection. The most sought-after natural thumb sticks are those with plenty of space for a thumb and a pair of perfectly matching forks growing at an equal angle from a straight parallel shank. A perfectly shaped natural thumb stick is surprisingly difficult to find. The bark on the illustration was damaged and was stripped off the shank, but it is a good example of a naturally formed thumb stick.

Some naturally grown sticks.

A CROSS-HEAD STICK

These shapes are often found in hedgerows that have been laid several years earlier or on fallen trees, causing shoots to grow vertically from a horizontal branch. Sometimes the principal branches of a tree spread out horizontally and a smaller branch grows from it in a perpendicular direction. Any of these circumstances can produce a cross-head stick; take time to observe where there is a horizontal branch growing. Providing you have permission, cut the appropriate (oversized) section from both the horizontal and vertical branches and allow the stick to fully season in its raw state.

Step 1. The handle of the stick is cut down to size and both ends are trimmed with a flat rasp to remove saw-cut marks; both ends of the handle are finished with 120 and 180g abrasive which will give an acceptable finish for this type of stick.

Step 2. Any protrusions from branches on the shank and handle are removed; use a flat or round rasp to smooth the lumps down to the shank. Use the 180g abrasives to smooth off any loose bark and lumps, taking care not to remove too much bark.

Step 3. Cut the shank to length using the junior hacksaw; prepare the tip to accept a rubber ferrule by gently rounding the edge of the tip. Examine the whole stick to make sure there are no obvious defects.

Step 4. Apply raw linseed oil to the whole stick using a small piece of lint-free cloth. More coats can be applied once the previous one has dried. Soak the cloth in soapy water before throwing it away as it may self-ignite. The dried oil can be burnished with a clean cloth to give the stick a pleasant sheen. Fit and glue a rubber ferrule onto the tip when all coats of oil have been applied and the stick is finished. The combination of oil and glue will help to seal the tip.

A KNOB STICK

Making a knob stick is slightly more difficult than the previous sticks, as more waste material has to be removed to form the knob handle. The shank has not been straightened on the stick, most of the time was taken removing the waste wood and shaping the knob so it blends in with the shank. Again, search woodland and hedgerows to locate a suitable piece of timber to make the knob and shank. A similar piece to the cross-handled stick may be suitable. Allow the stick to season before dressing it.

Step 1. Select an appropriately sized block with a branch of a suitable size.

Step 2. Cut off most of the surplus material using a sharp hand saw; if a saw is not available use a rasp, which will take longer. Shape the knob using rasps. This may take some time to complete depending on the amount of material to remove and type and size of rasp available.

Step 3. Continue shaping the knob until a smooth, comfortable finish is achieved and there is an even transition between the shank and handle. Use abrasives 120 and 180g to make a smooth finish on the knob handle. Smooth off the shank and fit a rubber ferrule. Finish the stick with a few coats of oil.

Apart from the seasoning period, the above sticks can be made quite quickly with a few basic tools. Please note that none of the sticks were straightened.

Small block stick.

Waste material being removed.

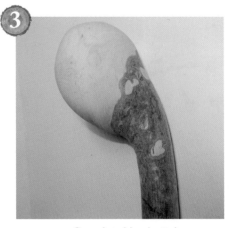

Completed knob stick.

Making one-piece market and crook sticks

Making market and crook sticks from one piece of timber is quite a challenge and they are much more difficult to make than the previous one-piece sticks featured, especially if you intend to cut and collect your own timber. The term 'block stick' is often used for this type as they are made from a substantial block of timber that is cut from a tree with a branch protruding at an appropriate angle from the block. The block forms the handle and the protruding branch becomes the shank.

Some woodland workers who regularly coppice overgrown woods are aware that stickmakers require 'blocks' and will cut them using chainsaws during coppicing projects. If you know a woodland worker it is well worth asking if they will cut block sticks for you; some keep a stock of blocks that are for sale. If you have permission to enter woodland to cut your own timber it is worth asking the owner or agent for consent to cut these larger block sticks, bearing in mind that a substantial section of a tree will be cut down.

Locating a large enough segment from a tree to make a handle for a market stick or shepherd's crook with a suitable branch projecting at the correct angle from it can be time-consuming and difficult to find. Once found the next task is to cut out the segment from the tree; a sharp saw is required to cut through the thicker branch. Few stickmakers carry chainsaws when they are foraging in woods, so generally resort to cutting all their timber with a pruning or bow saw. Before cutting through the heavier section, undercut it to prevent the timber from splitting as it falls to the ground. Take care when felling large segments from trees as they can abruptly fall to the ground in an unexpected direction with little warning. A substantial amount of a tree has to be felled in order to obtain a suitable block and there will be a lot of waste timber strewn around to deal with. When cutting the block section on site, ensure that it is long enough to reduce the risk of cracks materializing as the block dries out during seasoning. The final problem is carrying the heavy piece of timber from the wood back to your vehicle, especially if you have cut several shanks. Remember to tidy up the site before leaving.

Once at home, the block should be stored in a cool, dry environment and be allowed to season for a period of three or four years depending on the size, making it a longer-term project. It is worthwhile sealing the cut ends of the block to prevent it from drying too quickly, which may cause it to crack. Commercial wood sealants are available but applying some old varnish or paint will help to slow down the drying process and reduce the risk of the timber cracking.

An alternative method is to wrap the block in polythene, which slows the drying process. It is advisable to cut all your timber oversize in case cracks appear during the seasoning period. Ensure the timber is regularly treated against woodworm as it will be stored for a considerable period.

Freshly cut block sticks.

A seasoned block.

MAKING A PAIR OF 'BLOCK' STICKS

Avoid making a careless mistake while making these sticks. Remember that the block was difficult to obtain, it has taken several years to season and a careless mistake can quickly ruin the project. Allow plenty of time to consider every action.

Make a nose-in stick

Step 1. Choose an appropriately sized and seasoned block stick and check that there are no serious defects or infestation from pests in the block. Carefully cut off surplus timber equally from both sides of the block, leaving two flat sides that are aligned with the shank. The surplus material can be cut off with a sharp hand saw.

Step 2. Use a clear Perspex template to draw the shape of the handle on a flattened side, ensuring that the handle and the shank merge together to form an acceptable heel and crown. It will help when dressing the handle to draw the shape on the opposite side, making sure both shapes are perfectly opposite each other.

Step 3. Cut away surplus timber from the inside and outside lines of the handle; keep the edges close to but not crossing over the lines.

Step 4. When removing timber from the sides of the block handle, ensure they are aligned with the shank.

Step 5. With the handle cut to shape it is a good opportunity to remove any excess timber from both the flat sides, reducing the work required to dress the handle. Begin dressing using rasps to remove surplus material, removing equal amounts from both sides to maintain a balanced handle.

Remove surplus wood and flatten the sides.

Use a template to draw the handle shape.

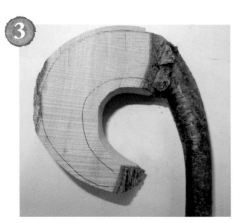

Cut off wood to the template.

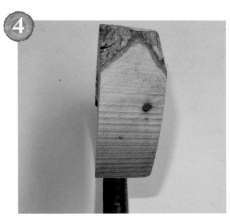

Reduce sides and align with shank.

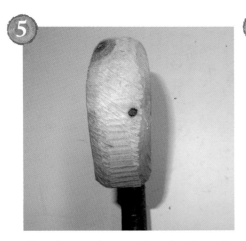

Start dressing keeping the sides aligned.

Straighten the shank near the handle.

49

Continue dressing the handle.

Sealer applied ready for finishing.

Step 6. Before commencing the final dressing of the handle, straighten the shank. Be careful not to damage the neck and heel section during the straightening process. It is not always possible to obtain a perfectly straightened shank if it is bent close to the heel because of the variable grain orientation.

Step 7. Having made the shank as straight as possible, continue to dress the handle ensuring that both sides remain equal.

Step 8. When the desired shape and size of the handle is achieved, smooth the surface using different grades of abrasives until you have an acceptable finish. Use fine rasps and abrasives to merge the shank with the handle, ensuring that there is a smooth progression between the two sections of the stick. Use sanding sealant to seal the timber before applying a finish of varnish or lacquer.

MAKE A SHEPHERD'S CROOK

Most of the steps to make a nose-out shepherd's crook are similar to those described for a nose-in market stick handle. In this sequence, some new tools and methods are introduced.

Step 1. Select a large seasoned block where the angle of the shank is set close to the block, so a nose-out crook form can be made. Note that the angle of the shank leaving the block differs slightly according to the type of handle to be made.

Step 2. Cut two flat sides on the block keeping them aligned with the shank; be aware that any misalignment on a larger crook handle will be exaggerated so ensure both cut sides are carefully aligned with the heel, crown and nose of the crook while removing surplus wood. The surplus timber can be cut off using a sharp hand saw. An alternative method is to use an electric planer, which removes thin shavings with each pass. This method provides more control than

Flattened sides using an electric planer.

a saw and is a good option to maintain alignment between the handle and shank; it also allows the sides to be tapered towards the nose a little more easily but it does create a lot of shavings to clean up.

Step 3. Use a Perspex template to draw the outline of the handle on the flattened sides ensuring the heel section merges into the shank. The positioning of the handle in relation to the shank is critical to the successful appearance of a crook; the crown of the crook must not droop, it should look as though it is standing slightly up. Copy the outline of the handle onto the opposite side ensuring it is carefully aligned with the original side. It is a good idea to make two or three datum marks to help with the alignment of both sides; small pilot holes can be drilled through the block at strategic points to aid the alignment. Mark the surplus timber by cross-hatching the areas to be removed.

Step 4. Cut away the surplus timber from the inside line first with a tool of your choice, this may be a band saw, an electric jig saw, a coping saw or a hand saw and wood chisels, leaving a little spare timber to allow for any adjustments. When wood from the inside line has been removed, cut away

Shape drawn using a template.

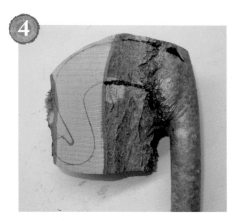

Remove surplus material.

the surplus timber from the outside line again leaving some spare timber for any minor adjustments.

Step 5. Before completing the dressing of the handle, straighten the shank. Having a straight shank helps to align it with the handle, and allows for any minor misalignment to be made before the dressing process is completed.

Step 6. Complete dressing the handle to size and shape using a range of tools such as rasps, carving chisels or knives. Initially concentrate on getting the correct shape on the inside line before tackling the outside line.

Step 7. Take care while forming the

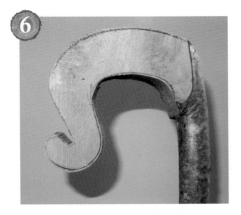

Dressing the crook handle.

turned-out nose. Remove a little material at a time and regularly check that the shape of the nose is balanced and is aligned with the crown and heel of the handle.

Step 8. When the ideal shape is achieved, use graded abrasives to smooth the handle so all marks and defects have been removed. Avoid using liquid abrasives as they are likely to stain the timber.

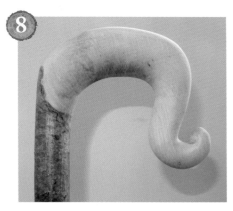

The handle dressed ready for sealing.

Step 9. Use sanding sealer to raise the grain and seal the timber, smooth the surface with fine abrasives. Use an additional coat of sealant if required;

Completed one-piece crook.

allow it to dry and test that a smooth surface has been achieved. Apply your preferred finish; apply several coats if required. It is advisable to de-nib the finish in between any additional coats so the new coats can adhere to the surface.

Making one-piece sticks using roots and contorted branches

Beautiful and unusual sticks can be made using roots and contorted branches for the handles. Searching places such as a copse or thicket, hedgerow, gutter or riverbank can reveal a host of shapes that are suitable for making one-piece sticks. With blackthorn thickets, select a suitable shank, follow it down into the ground and dig out the roots to determine if they are suitable to form a handle. The size and shape of the roots will vary considerably but it is possible to make interesting and attractive handles from the roots. Blackthorn is covered with sharp thorns that are toxic so it is important to wear appropriate protective clothing when cutting, collecting and working with these plants. Similarly; hazel and other species of trees can be found growing along banks of streams, brooks and rivers and over time flood waters have exposed the roots. Occasionally a potential shank can be found growing from one of these roots that will make a superb stick. Hedgerows are well worth searching, especially where a hedge has been cut and laid several years earlier. The horizontally laid sections often have sufficient material to make good handles and have upright shoots growing from them that will make excellent sticks. Seldom-used varieties of wood such as hawthorne, ash and wild rose can be found in hedgerows and copses and are suitable for stickmaking.

One-piece leg cleek.

Making a one-piece leg cleek

Follow the same steps used to make a full crook or nose-in stick described earlier. Cut off surplus timber from both sides of the block to form two flat sides that align with the shank. The waste can be removed using a hand saw or a portable electric planer. Use a template to mark the shape onto the flat sides ensuring that the shank blends into the handle, resulting in clean lines both inside and outside between the shank and handle. Cut out the shape of the handle carefully removing surplus wood from the inside and outside lines using a coping saw or jig saw, ensuring that a smooth transition is maintained between the handle and shank. Leave a little spare timber on each flat side and along the inside and outside lines to allow for any error that may occur during the shaping process. Shape the handle using rasps to remove excess material and ensure that the handle and shank blend well together, making a seamless connection. Avoid using coarse rasps too close to the inside and outside lines when shaping the handle as they may create deep marks that are difficult to remove.

Complete shaping the handle using abrasives in sequence, for example 80 grit then 100 grit to 120 to 150 and so on, until all scratches and marks are removed from the timber. When the shaping is complete, straighten the shank ensuring it remains aligned with the handle. Be aware that it is not always possible to remove severe bends that are positioned close to the heel due to the grain formation of the wood, so never force the shank and damage the stick at this stage. When satisfied that the handle and shank are aligned, finish the handle and remove any defects from the shank. Check the measurements of the handle ensuring that they are within allowable tolerances. Seal the timber with sanding sealer and when it is dry, apply a finish of your choice using several thin coats. When the finish has completely dried, check it for any minor defects and if satisfied give the stick a final polish. Fit a ferrule when the length of the stick is decided.

Please remember that permission must be obtained from the owner before cutting any material.

Chapter 8
Making Wooden-Handled Sticks

Wood is probably the most common choice of material for stick handles as so many shapes and styles can be made from a vast range of readily available timbers that make good-quality handles at a reasonable cost. Handles can be made from relatively small pieces of odd-shaped offcuts of timber that are often available at car boot sales, joinery businesses and timber merchants at minimal cost. If planked timber is preferred, it is available in a range of appropriate thicknesses for all types and styles of handles, giving stickmakers an enormous selection to choose from. Naturally contorted shaped timbers suitable for handles can also be found in hedgerows, woodland, parkland and gardens. If the opportunity arises it is worth checking any trees or bushes that have been cut or blown down – it is surprising how many potential handles can be found in these situations. Burrs are growths that form on trees causing the grain to intermingle, which make strong and attractive handles for sticks and are usually available from timber merchants in the form of planks. Most stickmaking suppliers will provide pre-cut handle shapes from different species of timber if you don't have the facilities or equipment to cut your own handle blanks.

Wooden sticks can be categorized into three principal groups; one-piece; two-piece and multi-piece. One-piece sticks have been dealt with in the previous chapter, leaving two and multi-piece wooden sticks as the featured topics in this chapter.

Two-piece sticks comprise of a handle and shank that are generally made from different types of wood, although there are exceptions where they are made separately using the same species of timber. In the case of a multi-piece stick it is usually the handle that is made from several different types and colours of wood to perhaps highlight specific features on a carved head, or simply to place contrasting colours in the handle. Occasionally a shank may be decorated with inlaid wooden segments. Several different methods are used in the following stickmaking projects to give examples of the various techniques that can be used to make wooden-handled sticks. Sometimes the techniques are repeated, so are not shown in the step-by-step guides to avoid duplication.

One consideration when jointing handles and shanks is whether to make straight or angled joints. During the following sequences, three-angled joints are made to help the reader see the difference between angles at five, ten and fifteen degrees. Angle joints help to prevent a handle from turning on a shank, which is beneficial in some situations, such as shepherding. Several different shapes and species of wooden handle blanks have been cut out to make some of the handles featured below.

A selection of timber blanks.

MAKING A LADIES' NOSE-IN WALKING STICK

Step 1. The handle blank used for this stick is a piece of London Plane.

Step 2. Begin shaping the handle by carefully rounding all the square edges; start on the inside line first. Use a rasp to round off the flat edges on both sides of the inside line of the handle; maintain the symmetry on both of the inside lines until a rounded surface is achieved. Continue to round off the corners on the outside lines of the handle.

Step 3. Carefully continue rounding and shaping both the inside and outside lines of the handle and shape the nose. Use 80 or 100 grit abrasives to remove any deep marks caused by using rasps.

Step 4. Mark the centre of handle and drill an 8mm hole to a depth of around $2^{1}/_{2}$ in (65mm) to take a piece of threaded rod.

Step 5. A five-degree angle joint is made between the handle and shank, which helps to give the plain stick a little more character. The angle is cut using the mitre fence on a sanding machine; both the handle and shank are cut at exactly the same angle. Note; an angle joint looks best when the angle slopes upwards towards the nose.

Step 6. Three jubilee clips and a pair of elasticated straps are used to hold the joint firmly together while the adhesive sets. This simple device is frequently used to hold a handle firmly onto a shank to ensure the joint has closed.

Step 7. When the adhesive has set, the handle can be merged onto the shank making sure that the inside line of the stick and shank follow a straight line. The outside line can slope outwards a

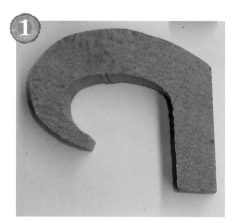

Selected London Plane blank.

Start shaping the handle.

Continue dressing the handle.

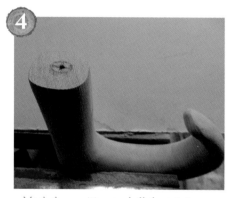

Mark the position to drill the joint peg.

A five-degree angle cut onto the handle.

Handle smoothed to merge with the shank.

The completed nose-in walker.

little towards the crown of the handle. Use smoother rasps and abrasives in sequence to remove all marks and to make a smooth surface in preparation for sanding sealer and a finish of your choice. Fit a ferrule if the length of the stick is known.

Step 8. Apply sanding sealer to the handle and shank to raise the grain and seal the wood. Smooth off the sealed surfaces with a fine abrasive (240 grit) and apply a finish of your choice.

MAKING A CARDIGAN-HANDLED STICK

Step 1. Two useful stick handles can be made from quite a small block of timber. The two shapes are drawn onto the block of wood so that the grain of the wood is in the best position. A Perspex template is used to aid in marking out the shapes.

Step 2. A market stick and a cardigan stick handle shape are cut from the block using a band saw. Waste timber is kept to a minimum. The cardigan shape is used for this project.

Step 3. The outline of the cardigan handle is cut from the block. The arrow drawn onto the block shows the direction of the grain. The weakest part of the timber is between the joint and the heel, which will be strengthened by using a threaded rod to make the joint; the length of threaded rod will be sufficient to go from the base of the joint to the corner of the heel.

Step 4. Begin shaping the handle by rounding off the sharp corners as described earlier, start on the inside line to maintain the correct shape of the handle.

Step 5. Continue dressing the handle using rasps and a range of abrasives. A fifteen-degree angled joint has been made on the handle and shank and is cut using the mitre table on a sanding machine. Angled joints can also be accurately cut using a mitre saw that has the facility for setting a range of angles. The steel ruler shows the angle of the joint pointing towards the nose of the stick.

Step 6. Check the accuracy of the joint before gluing the handle onto the shank; firmly hold the handle onto the shank using the elasticated straps until the glue has set. On some joints, it is a good idea to mark the handle and shank at the point of the best fit.

Step 7. Before completing shaping the handle and marrying the handle and shank together it is a good idea to wrap some masking tape around the shank to protect it from rasp, file or abrasive marks during the merging process.

Step 8. Dress the handle using rasps, files and abrasives to make a smooth joint and surface in readiness for sealing and finishing with a product of your choice.

Two handle shapes drawn on a blank.

Two handles cut from a blank.

Cardigan handle outline showing grain direction.

Begin rounding off the handle.

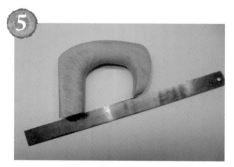

A fifteen-degree angled joint.

Check the fit of the joint.

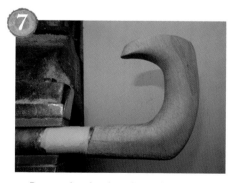

Protect the shank with masking tape.

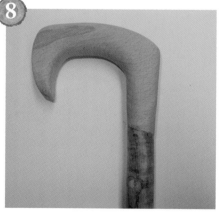

Dress the handle and prepare it for finishing.

MAKING A LEG CLEEK

Step 1. A Perspex former is used as the template to draw the outline of the handle onto a piece of burr elm; the shape was cut out using a band saw.

Step 2. Because the inside line of the handle is quite tight it is difficult to use a rasp to round off the sharp edges so a rotary cutter was used as an option to remove surplus material. These cutters are very aggressive and must be used with care. It is recommended that safety glasses and gloves are worn to protect your eyes and hands, and also advisable to wear a mask or have a powerful dust extractor to prevent inhaling dust from the cutters.

Step 3. Continue dressing the handle using the rotary cutter, rasps, files and abrasives until the handle is ready for fitting onto the shank. A ten-degree angled joint has been cut on the handle and shank using a sanding machine to form both the angles accurately. The joint is held together using jubilee clips and elasticated bungies.

Step 4. When the adhesive has set, continue dressing the handle keeping the inside line aligned with the shank. A leg cleek is the only handle where there are recognized measurements; therefore ensure that the crown loop measures the same as an old penny and the gape measures the same as an old halfpenny. These measurements are important if you intend to enter your sticks in any BSG competitions.

Step 5. On completion of the shaping, smooth the surface of the handle and shank using a range of abrasives, seal the timber with a sanding sealer and apply a finish of your choice.

Cut out the shape of the leg cleek.

Edges being rounded with a rotary cutter.

Use jubilee clips and bungies to hold the joint tight.

Dress the handle to comply with measurements.

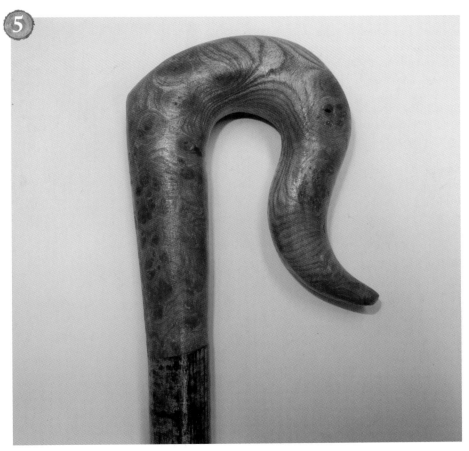

Apply a sealer and a finish of your choice.

MAKING A SHEPHERD'S CROOK

Step 1. Two shapes, a shepherd's crook and nose-in market handle were cut out of a small plank of dark patterned timber. The shepherd's crook blank will be used for this project.

Step 2. Begin rounding the sharp edges, again start along the inside lines ensuring the crook shape is maintained throughout the process.

Step 3. Woodwork rasps can be used on larger blanks to round off and form the outline shape of the handle; they will remove surplus timber quite quickly and safely with careful use. Rotary machines with suitable burrs can be used to shape handles if preferred.

Step 4. The crook handle is roughly shaped and is being prepared for fitting onto the chestnut shank.

Step 5. Use a washer to determine the best position to drill the hole for the studding jointing peg. Mark the centre of the hole onto the base of the neck ready for drilling.

Step 6. An 8mm threaded rod is used to join the handle to the dark chestnut shank. The rod is about 5in (250mm) long with roughly equal sections in the handle and shank. A flat joint has been made, as it is unlikely to be used as a working stick.

Step 7. The handle and shank are glued together using a slow-setting epoxy adhesive, held in place using jubilee clips and elasticated bungies during the setting period of the epoxy. The slower-setting epoxy is stronger than the faster-setting adhesive.

Step 8. When the adhesive has fully set,

Two shapes cut out of a blank.

Rounding the inside and outside lines.

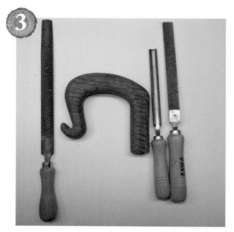

Using woodworking rasps to shape.

The crook handle shaped.

Use a washer to determine the best position.

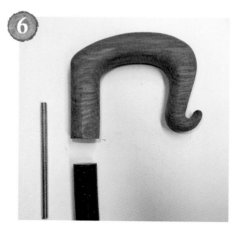

Threaded rod is used to make the joint.

Handle held in place.

Dress the handle to make a smooth joint.

Check the handle is aligned with the shank.

continue dressing the handle ensuring the inside line of the neck and shank are aligned. The outside line of the neck can be allowed to lean outwards slightly, which helps to make the handle have the appearance that it stands up rather than drooping.

Step 9. Before sealing and finishing the handle, make any adjustments to ensure that the nose, crown heel and neck are perfectly aligned. When satisfied, seal and finish the complete stick with your choice of product.

Making multi-piece sticks

Multi-piece sticks are less common; several pieces of timber are used to make the handles, especially when a carved feature is used for decoration. Sets of differently coloured wooden discs can be mounted on a curved round bar and glued together to form a handle. Different coloured woods are often used on turned handles. Shanks are generally made from a single piece of wood as too many joints will make the shank vulnerable to failure. A simple example of using multi-pieces of timber is to make a handle using plywood.

MAKING A PLYWOOD-HANDLED STICK

Step 1. An offcut of good-quality 1in (25mm) thick plywood sheet is cut into two equal parts.

Step 2. A piece of black veneer is placed between the two sections of plywood to highlight the division between both sides of the finished handle.

Step 3. Using good-quality wood adhesive, spread a thin, even film over the surfaces of the plywood and veneer and firmly clamp the sections together. Allow the glue to set for at least twenty-four hours before releasing the clamps.

Step 4. With the clamps removed, use a Perspex template to mark out the shapes for four handles (or as many as will fit) onto one side of the double plywood block. With a block of wood this size a variety of handle shapes can be made.

Step 5. With a band saw, cut out the four handle shapes from the double block of plywood. In this project, there are two nose-in handles and two crook shapes with turned-out noses.

Step 6. A nose-in shape is to be used for this project. The three remaining handles will be used in later projects. The edges are rounded off on a pair of handles using woodworking rasps. The inside line is used for making the principal shape of the handle.

Step 7. With the handle shape established, it is being prepared for joining onto a spiral shank. A piece of 8mm threaded rod is used to make the joint.

Step 8. To help set off the black veneer that is running through the centre of the handle, a black spacer is placed

Plywood sheet cut into two pieces.

Insert black veneer between plywood sheets.

The plywood pieces clamped and glued together.

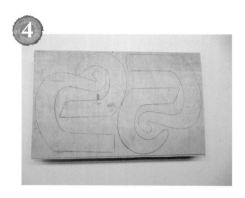

Draw handle shapes onto plywood.

Four shapes cut from plywood.

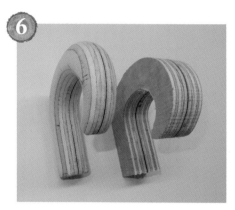

Begin shaping a pair of handles.

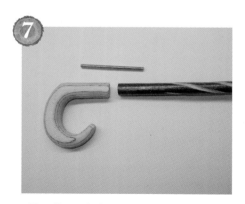

Handle ready for jointing onto a shank.

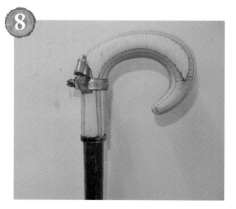

Black spacer fitted between handle and shank.

Handle dressed and ready for finishing.

The finished plywood handle.

between the handle and shank which will make an attractive feature on the stick.

Step 9. The handle and shank with the black spacer glued together. The handle shape is complete and is ready for the final finishing.

Step 10. The plywood handle is finished and jointed onto a spiral cut shank, making an attractive and unusual stick from an offcut of plywood. It is important to use good-quality plywood for handles as there is less risk of gaps appearing between the layers.

MAKING TURNED HANDLES

If you own a wood lathe it is quite easy to make some simple knob handles from short pieces of squared timber. Another option is to use a series of flat wooden pieces of different species and colour to make a multi-piece handle. Use offcuts of timber to make an interesting range of handles. Glue several flat pieces of wood together and clamp them tightly until the glue has set to make a solid piece of sufficient length to make a knob handle. With a lathe, spigots can be accurately turned to accept a plain or beaded collar on any turned handle. If a rolled collar is permanently fastened onto a shank, several turned handles can be made which can be interchanged, giving the user a choice of handles.

Step 1. Select a piece of square timber about 2in (50mm) square x 6in (150mm) long. The timber can be thicker and longer if required. Locate the centre on each end and drill an 8mm diameter hole in both about $2^1/_2$in deep (this can be done on the lathe). Glue a length of 8mm threaded rod in each end, leaving about $2^1/_2$in protruding to fit into a shank.

Step 2. Cut the block into two equal lengths to enable two handles to be made from the piece.

Step 3. Hold a block by the threaded rod in a chuck mounted on the lathe. Turn a spigot on the end next to the threaded rod for a collar. The spigot diameter is turned to suit the inside diameter of a collar of your choice; it needs to be a neat fit with the collar.

Step 4. Remove the handle from the chuck and slip the collar onto the turned spigot to check that it fits. Next turn the shape of the handle ensuring that the neck merges perfectly with the outside diameter of the collar. Allow a fraction of overhang for the final sanding.

Step 5. With the neck turned to fit exactly with the collar, continue turning the handle to your chosen shape. Use a range of abrasives to smooth the surface. Apply sanding sealer to raise the grain and when dry, use a fine abrasive to smooth the surface. This process may be repeated until a perfect surface is achieved.

Step 6. Continue until the handle fits the collar perfectly and an acceptable finish is achieved.

Step 7. Glue the collar in position using a wing nut and washer to hold it in place until the adhesive has set. With the collar fixed, the handle can be fitted to a shank of your choice.

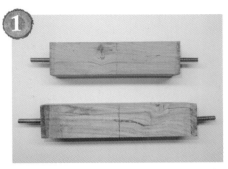

A pair of blocks with threaded rod glued in each end.

The pair of blocks cut into two.

Turned spigot for the collar.

Handle turned to fit the collar.

Complete turning the handle.

Finish the handle.

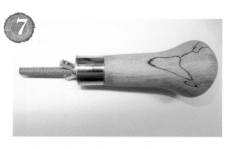

Secure the collar until the glue sets.

handle spigots must be identical in size. In the example shown a threaded (8mm) insert is fitted into a hazel shank and a rolled collar fitted and glued onto the shank. The turned handles are made with a short spigot that fits inside the rolled collar giving a close-fitting joint.

There is no limit to the number of handles that can be interchanged with a single shank, especially when a rolled collar is used. A number of clients enjoy owning and using sticks with interchangeable handles; the sticks are unusual and little quirky.

Step 8. Cut a spigot onto a straightened shank and fit the handle. Dress the shank and complete the stick.

Use an old snooker cue

In keeping with the turned theme, an old turned snooker cue handle extension section can be used to make a shank. Minor adjustments may be required to fit into the collar.

An endless range of turned handle shapes can be made using a lathe; some

A variety of turned handles.

examples are shown here. Most of these handles were made from small offcuts of timber. The two handles on the right of the image are made from a mixture of timbers that were glued together.

Interchangeable handles

Turned handles can be made interchangeable by fixing a rolled collar onto a shank. A rolled collar will cope with slight differences in the diameter of the handles; with a straight collar the

A snooker cue used as a stick.

Insert and rolled collar fitted.

A selection of interchangeable handles.

MAKING A PAIR OF DUCK HANDLES

The purpose of the project is to make a matching pair of handles and it was decided to make a pair of short walking sticks with duck heads. The heads are decorated using a pyrography tool and nibs; there is no colouring added other than that caused by the hot nibs. An option is to paint and colour the handles to make a male and female head. It is recommended that you obtain some clearly detailed photos of duck heads to help in making the feather patterns, especially around the eyes and the inside of neck.

Step 1. Select a piece of planked timber large enough to make two heads. Mark out the outline of both heads on the timber and cut out the shapes using your preferred method.

Step 2. Paper or cardboard templates can be made so that the same sizes and shapes are transferred onto both of the wooden blanks. Drawings and photos of birds and animals can be obtained from books or from websites. Use the templates to draw the outline onto the wooden blanks and mark some datum points, such as the position of the eyes and the position where the bill joins the head.

Step 3. The basic shapes of the heads are fashioned using rasps and carving knives and the eye positions have been drilled to give datum points for reference during the decorating sequence. Angled joints and a threaded rod are used to fix the handles onto the shanks.

Step 4. Small handles can be difficult to hold when decorating them, so a useful option is to glue a section of threaded rod into the handle and fix it into a round bar with a tapped thread. The two heads in this project have angled joints so disposable spacers were made to fit between the handles and round bars. This allows the heads to be held by the rods in a vice at the most appropriate position or angle for working and dressing without damaging them. Both the heads have been shaped and the necks brought down to their approximate size; these will be finished when the heads are attached to the shanks.

Step 5. Finish shaping both the heads while they are attached to the round bars, leaving the joint area until the shanks are attached. It is important that smooth surfaces on both the heads are prepared for the pyrography process. An uneven or lumpy surface will make pyrography more difficult and will spoil the finished appearance. Begin by burning in the outline of where the beak

meets the head, followed by detailing the upper and lower sections of the bill. Start cutting in the small feathers from the beak, working towards the rear of the head. The feathers nearest the beak are tiny and can be represented by a series of thin, short lines close together; as you approach the eyes the feathering needs to flow around the eye sockets.

Step 6. Continue burning the feathers, following the contour of the head from the beak to the back of the head and down the neck. The size of the feathers increases as you move towards the base of the neck. Stop burning the feathers a short distance away from the joints, as the handles will be reduced in diameter to fit the shank.

Step 7. Join and glue the handles onto the shanks ensuring a neat close-fitting joint is achieved between the angled faces.

Step 8. Reduce the handle necks down so they merge with the shanks, smooth the surface of the necks before continuing with the pyrography detailing. Complete the pyrography down to the line of the joints. Note that the size of the feathers increases as the neck approaches the body.

Step 9. Set and fix a pair of glass eyes in each head using an epoxy putty.

A pair of head shapes cut from a plank.

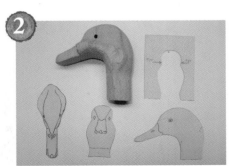
Make cardboard templates.

Angled joints cut and threaded rod glued into handles.

4

Disposable spacers used to help when shaping the handles.

5

Start the pyrography sequence.

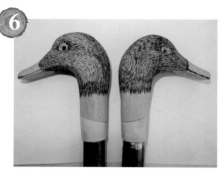

6

Pyrography almost complete.

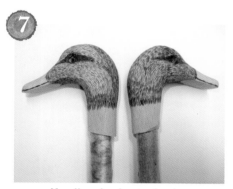

7

Handles glued onto shanks.

8

Joints and handles dressed.

9

Eyes fitted and heads sealed ready for the final finish.

Carefully remove any excess putty from around the eyes. When the putty has fully set, very carefully finish pyrography around the eyes. Use a fine brass or wire brush and gently brush away any particles of dust from the pyrography carving on the heads and using a fine abrasive (400 grit), gently smooth off the surface of the heads. Use a soft bristle brush to remove any dust caused by the abrasive and then seal the handles with a sanding sealer.

Step 10. This step is optional. The handles may be painted to represent a male and female duck using colouring of your choice. Neither of the ducks in this project have been painted, the colour is achieved by burning alone. The handles and shanks are finished with several coats of thinned varnish.

MAKING A PAIR OF SPANIEL HEADS

Step 1. Mark out and cut three spaniel head profiles from a block of planed timber. It is surprising how many handle shapes can be made from a small offcut. The outline of the heads can be drawn onto each blank as a guide for shaping.

Step 2. Insert and glue a section of threaded rod into the base of the handle.

When the glue has set, the handle can be screwed into a section of hexagonal steel so it can be firmly held in a vice at different angles. Begin shaping the handles using the outline drawn earlier. A pair of carving knives are used to remove most of the surplus timber. When using very sharp tools, it is recommended that safety gloves are worn to protect the hands from severe cuts if a knife should slip.

Step 3. Continue shaping the head using knives, rasps and abrasives leaving sufficient material to join the handle onto a shank. Add the head details – eyes, ears, nose and mouth – using knives and chisels. Rotary machines can be used if preferred.

Step 4. When the details are complete, smooth off the surface and begin to pyrograph the ears. The fur on a spaniel's ears is generally quite long and wavy, so

Cut three profiles from a plank.

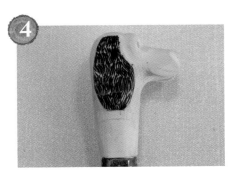

Using carving knives to begin shaping the heads.

Continue shaping one of the heads.

Begin pyrographing the ears.

Pyrographing is almost complete on one head.

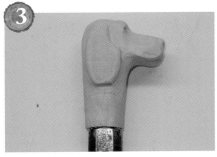

A pair of spaniels in progress.

A pair of spaniels painted and fitted onto shanks.

use fairly long and wavy strokes to replicate the fur.

Step 5. Following the ears, begin to pyrograph the head, begin at the nose and follow the contours of the head down towards the joint. Sweep the fur around the eye sockets, replicate the shorter fur near the nose and lengthen the strokes of the pen to reproduce the long hair around the neck of the dog. The noses can be burnt using pyrography nibs on a

higher setting if a dark finish without painting is required.

Step 6. The pair of spaniel heads' fur is carved using pyrography nibs. The eyes are inserted and fixed in place with epoxy putty. The neck section near the joint is unfinished; it will be finished when the handle is joined onto the shank.

Step 7. The heads are jointed and are merged with the shanks. The pyrography stops before the joint, leaving a short section of natural wood. The pyrographed sections of the head are painted, one black and white and one brown and white as requested by a client.

Step 8. Both the sticks were finished with several thinned coats of acrylic lacquer on the heads and shanks.

MAKING A PAIR OF DOGS ON A THUMB STICK

Step 1. Cut the thumb stick handle profile from a plank of timber using either a jig saw or a band saw. Note that a pair of blanks were cut from the plank; one will be used later.

Step 2. The outlines of the dogs were drawn onto the blanks, eye positions were drilled to make datum points for the carving. Using carving chisels or knives, carve the outline of the pair of dogs. If it is intended to carve a particular breed of dogs, try to obtain photos so their characteristics can be included in the carvings.

Step 3. With the outline complete, begin adding details to the ears, eyebrows, eye sockets and nose using small chisels and/or rotary carving tools.

Step 4. Continue detailing both heads and ensure that the section for the thumb is of sufficient width and is carved and smooth, so the handle is functional and comfortable to use.

Step 5. With the thumb section shaped, continue dressing the handle. Smooth off all sections of the handle that are not decorated and define the detailed sections of the heads. Detailing of the ears is complete and undecorated sections are smoothed ready for finishing.

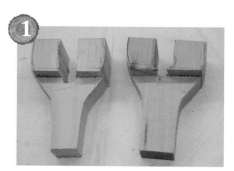
Thumb stick blanks cut out.

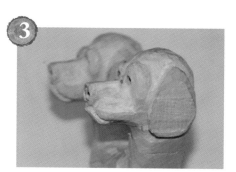
The outline shape of the dogs carved.

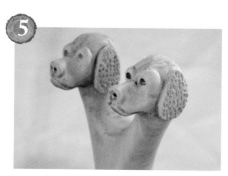
Add details to the heads.

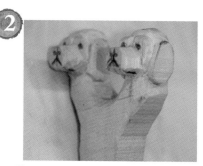
View from the front of the thumb stick.

Detailing nearing completion.

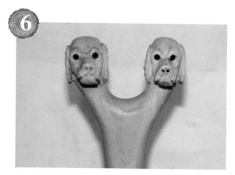
Eyes fitted into both heads.

Step 6. Fit a pair of eyes, ensuring that they are in line looking from the front and above; complete dressing the remaining parts of the head.

Step 7. Fix the completed head onto a shank and complete dressing the neck so it merges neatly with the shank. Seal the shank and handle and finish with a product of your choice.

Head finished and fitted onto shank.

MAKING A DOG HOLDING A PHEASANT

The timber selected for this project is oak, which is quite difficult to carve with hand tools, therefore a substantial amount of the detailed work was undertaken using rotary tools.

Step 1. Cut out the basic shape from a piece of planked timber.

Step 2. Mark a centre line around the whole profile; the line will help to maintain the carving in a centralized position throughout the project.

Step 3. Draw the outline of the dog and bird on each side of the block; highlight the high points to remind you not to remove any material from the points during the initial carving.

Step 4. Begin carving out the low points of the timber using sharp chisels or rotary tools; avoid cutting into any of the marked high points.

Step 5. Continue carefully removing timber from the lowest points in the carving. Position the eye sockets and begin shaping the dog's jaws around the bird. Start shaping the outline of the bird's head.

Step 6. On the opposite side of the carving, start to detail the shape of the dog's ear and the tail of the bird; again avoid removing any material from the marked high points.

Step 7. Carefully continue shaping the features on the left side of the handle and begin to add details; do not cut into any of the high points.

Step 8. Go to the opposite side of the head and continue carefully shaping the dog and bird and add more and more detail.

Step 9. Very carefully continue adding details to the dog's mouth, ears and nose. Begin to detail the head and wing feathers on the bird, add the position of the bird's eyes. Begin to detail some of the high points on the dog and bird. Most of this detail work is completed using fine rotary cutters.

Step 10. Slowly improve the detail on the whole carving and complete the work on all the high points. A distinguishing point between the dog's head and neck can be made if required or the neck can be tapered in readiness to be jointed onto the shank.

Step 11. The dog's eyes have been inserted and fixed in position. The neck is shaped to fit the shank. The final details to the dog and bird are complete and the whole handle surface has being smoothed and the dust removed from the carving before sealing the timber with cellulose sanding sealer.

Step 12. The carved head is complete and fitted onto a shank. The head and shank have had several coats of lacquer. In hindsight, the dog's ears could have been longer.

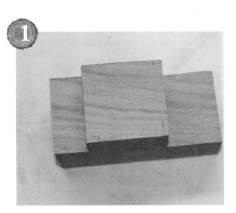

Basic shape cut out.

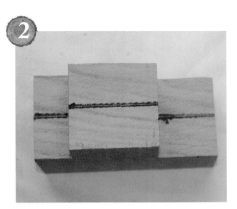

Draw a centre line.

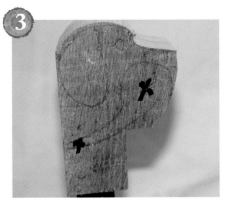

Draw the outline and highlight high points to avoid.

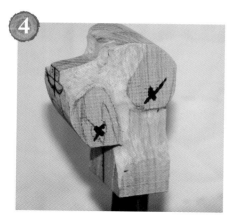

Begin carving the low points.

Position the eyes and mouth.

Begin shaping the dog's ears and the bird's tail.

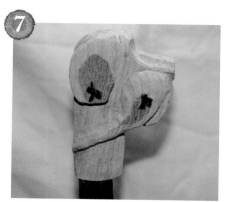

Detailing one side of the head.

Detailing the opposite side.

Eyes fitted, carefully adding more detail.

Improving the level of detail.

Detail completed, eyes fitted and the head sealed.

The completed carving of a dog with a pheasant.

MAKING A SPIRAL SHANK

An attractive style of shank is one with a spiral pattern cut into the timber. Spirals can be cut onto a parallel or a tapered piece of timber, which can be turned on a lathe. Old snooker cues or broom handles and dowelling can be used. Spirals can also be cut onto a natural shank and are effective when cut into a shank with a dark bark. Cutting spirals too deep will weaken the shank, so they are not recommended for use on frequently-used working sticks as they may crack. The basic tools required for this project are a pencil, ruler, a long, straight edge and a couple of sharp, round rasps with different diameters, masking tape and some fairly fine abrasive.

Step 1. Select a seasoned and straightened shank with a dark bark ensuring that the bark is sound and will not peel off the shank during the cutting procedure. Remove any offshoots and smooth them off. Leave a distance of about 8in (200mm) between both ends of the spiral.

Step 2. Wrap a couple of turns of masking tape around the shank with a gap of 3in (75mm) between the centres of each piece of tape. Draw a ring around the first piece of tape then measure 3in (75mm) and draw a circle around the second ring. Repeat this process along the shank ensuring that the distance between each ring is exactly 3in (75mm).

Step 3. On the largest end of the shank, mark three equal divisions so it looks like an equal 'Y'. Fasten the shank in a vice so it doesn't move, use a straight edge to mark a straight line along the shank starting from one of the legs of the 'Y' and call this line number 1. Turn the shank in the vice and repeat this process

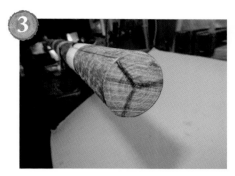

Dividing the shank into thirds.

for each 'Y' section, resulting in three straight lines numbered 1, 2 and 3 that intersect with the marked rings on each circle of masking tape.

Step 4. Draw a line using a pencil or a marking pen starting from the number 1 pencil line on the first ring of tape and join it to line number 2 on the second ring of tape. Next continue the line until it joins with line number 3 on the third ring. Continue drawing the line and join it to line 1 on the fourth ring; follow the sequence until the final ring is reached. You will now have an equally marked spiral line along the shank. It is recommended that only one heavy line is drawn at a time to avoid confusion.

Mark the first spiral along the shank.

Step 5. Using a small, round rasp, begin cutting the first spiral into the shank. Begin at the top end of the shank and guide the rasp, carefully following the

Cut out the first spiral.

drawn line until the last ring is reached. Initially make a very shallow cut and steer the rasp to meet each intersection point accurately. It is important that the masking tape rings are left in place until all the spirals have been cut out with a rasp.

Step 6. With the initial shallow spiral cut complete, mark out the second line beginning from the first ring down to the last, ensuring it remains parallel with the first spiral. Use a small rasp to make a shallow cut along the length of the second spiral. Draw in the last line and make a shallow spiral cut along the shank.

Mark and then cut out the second and third spirals.

Step 7. Begin to deepen the spiral cuts along the length taking care to match the start and finish points by gently leading the cut into and out of the spirals. Providing a sharp rasp is used, the sides

Use a sharp rasp to make a clean finish to the spirals.

of the spirals will have a clean finish; the overall finish can be improved by gently rubbing the inside of the spirals and the edges with a fine abrasive and using sanding sealer to protect the shank until it is fitted with a handle.
(Note; *see* earlier in this chapter for an example of a spiral shank fitted onto a plywood handle.)

A graduated or a tighter spiral can be achieved by changing the distance between the circular marks. On a second shank, graduated distances were used between the sets of rings beginning with a distance of 2in (50mm) at the top of the shank and increasing each pair of spirals by in (6mm) until the last ring was reached at the bottom of the shank. The result was very effective, with the tighter spirals at the top of the shank and opening out towards the bottom. The last part of this project is to fit a suitable handle onto the spiral shank.

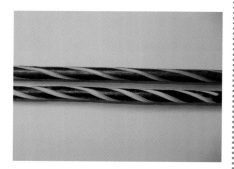

A pair of shanks with graduated spirals.

MAKING A TWO-PIECE MARKET STICK

The handle in the following example is made from a piece of burr elm. The shank is hazel.

Step 1. Use a template to copy the outline shape of the handle onto the burr, and cut out the desired shape. In the example the shape was cut out using a band saw. Select a suitable seasoned and straightened shank that will enhance the appearance of the burr handle.

Step 2. Drawing a centre line around the blank will help to maintain an even shape while forming the handle. Begin shaping the handle using rasps, taking care not to create deep marks in the wood. Work from both sides of the blank so the handle is even; leave a small amount of surplus wood on the handle until it is joined onto the shank.

Step 3. When the handle shape is formed, mark the best position to insert a peg into the base of the heel for the shank joint. A piece of 8mm diameter studding will be used for the joint. A 25mm diameter washer with an 8mm hole is ideal for locating the most suitable position to insert the peg.

Step 4. Make sure that the surface of the joint is perfectly flat so a close joint is made between the handle and shank. (The joint can be cut at an angle if preferred.) Drill an 8mm diameter hole to a depth of about $2^1/_2$ in (65mm) into the handle making sure it is perfectly true so the shank and handle will be accurately aligned.

Step 5. Cut a piece of 8mm mild steel threaded studding about 5in (125mm) long and using a suitable adhesive, glue it into the handle ensuring it is perfectly

aligned with the inside line of the handle. Remove surplus glue especially from the flat surface so it does not impede making a close joint.

Step 6. Check that your chosen shank is straightened and is a good match with the handle. Use the washer to mark the best position to drill an 8mm hole in the shank, and drill to a depth of $2^1/_2$in (65mm) again making sure the hole is correctly aligned with the handle. Ensure the end of the shank is perfectly flat so it fits closely to the handle. Wrap masking tape around the shank to (a) protect it from excess glue, and (b) enable an identification mark to be made.

Step 7. Fit the handle and shank together to test the alignment, turn the shank on the heel of the handle until the best position is found; with a pencil, mark a line on both the handle and tape showing the best position for aligning the joint. When satisfied that the alignment and the joint are good, glue the shank onto the handle maintaining pressure on the joint until the adhesive has set.

Step 8. When the glue has set, complete shaping the handle so that it merges perfectly onto the shank, ensuring the inside line of the handle and shank are aligned. Remove all marks from the handle using abrasives in sequence from coarse to fine, taking care not to damage the bark on the shank.

Step 9. Finish the shank, remove any loose bark and smooth off any offshoot stubs, ensure that the shank is straight and aligned with the handle; remove any bends. Providing the length of the shank is known, fit a ferrule – otherwise leave a longer shank that can be shortened later. With the shank and handle complete, apply sanding sealer to both; apply further coats if necessary.

Step 10. When the sealer is completely dry, smooth off all surfaces with a very fine abrasive. To finish the sticks, apply three coats of varnish in dry, dust-free conditions.

Cut out a market stick shape.

Begin shaping the handle.

Use a washer to help position the peg.

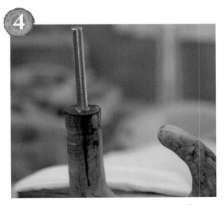

The studding glued into the handle.

Use masking tape to protect the shank.

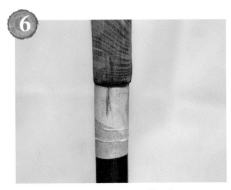

Mark the best position for the joint.

Handle fitted onto the shank.

Prepare the handle for finishing.

Apply varnish and complete the stick.

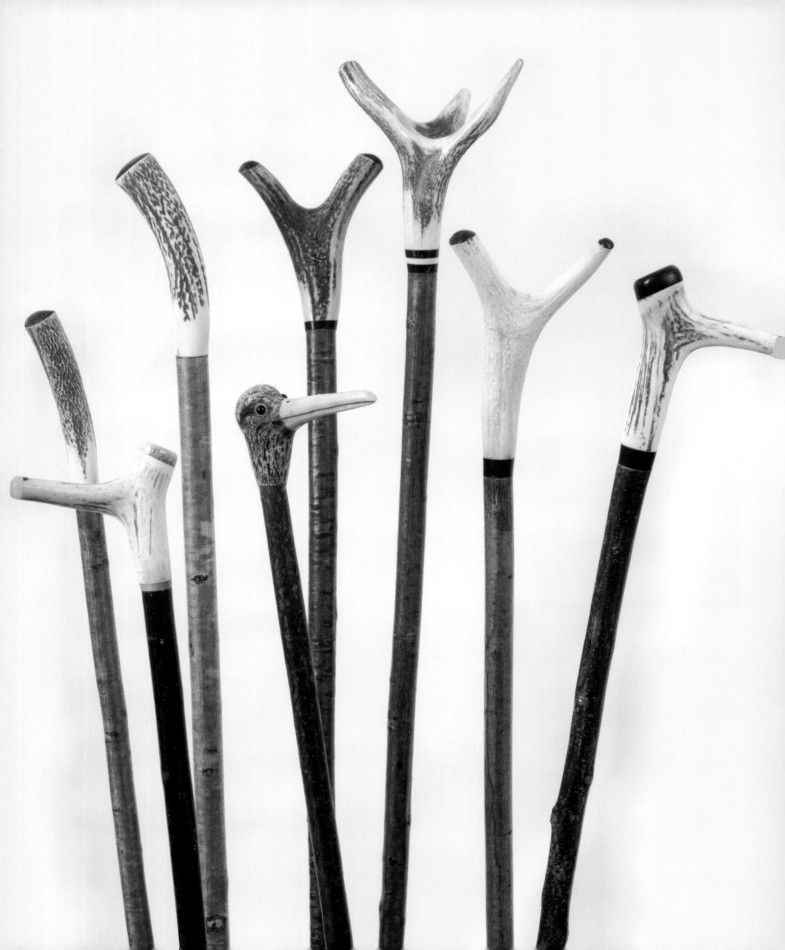

Chapter 9
Making Antler Sticks

Sticks made with antler handles are very popular for several reasons. They make good-quality, attractive and hard-wearing sticks that will last the user for many years. Many traditional users prefer a natural antler handle without any changes to the antler; they often choose a natural twisty shank to complement the antler shape and finally look for an oil finish rather than varnish or lacquer on the shank. Others prefer an antler that has been cleaned and even bleached to remove all traces of dirt and grime. From a stickmaker's perspective, antler is a good product to use. It is readily available, although prices are rising due to its popularity as dog chews. A serviceable, appealing and long-lasting stick can be made quickly with a few tools. Several shapes are available to suit a range of customers such as thumb sticks, staffs and a crown and tine.

Antler handles can be enhanced by attaching caps to the tips and fitting a matching spacer between the shank and antler. A popular option with antler is to encapsulate an object in clear resin in the antler crown, typically trout-fishing flies, bullets, military badges and buttons are encased in the clear resin. Antler is a hard material but with

modern rotary carving machines and burrs it can be successfully carved; many interesting, enthralling and amusing handles are made from antler. There are four main species of deer living in the United Kingdom; fallow, red, roe and sika. They all grow antlers, which can be used by stickmakers with varying degrees of success.

Fallow deer

Fallow deer are widespread in England and Wales, they can often be seen grazing leisurely in large private parks. They are the only breed to have palmate antlers; the palmate section is fairly flat and wide and is of little use to stickmakers. However, the antler can produce a useable coronet and tine that will make a suitable handle and occasionally a decent thumb stick can be obtained from these antlers. While the palmate section is not ideal for making stick handles, it can be used to make decorative mounts for candle holders, clocks, barometers and so on, so do not discard it. Craft workers will often find a use for the palmate sections and may be willing to make a swap with something useful for stickmaking.

Red deer

Many red deer roam wild, living on remote moorland and large estates which are owned by landowners who employ keepers and estate managers to control their numbers. Part of the management strategy is to cull old, injured and excess animals and the sport of 'stalking' provides a much-needed income to help the owners to provide the resources required to manage and maintain the herds of deer. Some estate owners provide food for the deer in extreme winter weather to maintain the animals in good condition, as many are farmed for their meat – venison. Red deer are common in Scotland, the Lake District, East Anglia, the New Forest and the south west of England and they are steadily spreading into other regions where controlled culling takes place. Red deer antlers, especially naturally cast ones make excellent handles and are frequently used by stickmakers. Antlers suitable for stickmaking are readily available from a number of suppliers.

Roe deer

Roe deer are widespread across the UK. These deer can often be seen in forests, woodland and farmland and occasionally in close proximity to towns and villages. Like red deer, numbers have to be controlled and excessive numbers are culled by gamekeepers and forest rangers. The antlers are plentiful but they are small. The surface of the antler is very rough and sharp, making them uncomfortable to hold. Small thumb sticks can be made from the antlers but it is difficult to make a neat joint between the antler and shank.

Sika deer

Sika deer are fairly common in Scotland, and their numbers are steadily increasing in some English counties, especially those containing large areas of woodland and forests. Sika deer sizes are in between the red and roe species; their antlers are smaller and have eight points. The antlers are more difficult to obtain than red deer although they make excellent handles as they have less pith, making some of them suitable for carving. If the opportunity arises, try to obtain some.

The illustration shows antlers from different breeds of deer.

Deer cast their antlers once a year, generally in spring, except for the roe deer which cast theirs in autumn. Cast antlers are difficult to find in the open countryside, although some are collected by experienced rangers who know the best places to find them. Deer are increasing around the country and the herds are causing so much damage to woodland and crops that they are being culled in order to contain manageable numbers. Deer stalking remains a popular sport throughout the UK but particularly in the large estates of the Scottish Highlands and islands, where the sport is a major contributor to the local economies. Gamekeepers and rangers responsible for managing the herds of deer select the old, injured or those in poor condition to be shot during shooting seasons; these antlers are a major source of material for stickmakers.

The popularity of venison is increasing, causing the expansion of deer farming, which in turn makes more antlers available for stickmakers. The size and thickness of antlers vary with the age of the animal; its location and feeding habits also contribute to the growth rate. There is evidence to suggest that where grazing is sparse, the antlers grow more slowly but are thicker than animals reared on lush grazing where the antler grows faster, resulting in thinner walls. The smaller, thicker-walled antlers are best for stickmaking and are generally found in wild deer that roam over the remote countryside rather than farmed deer contained in parkland. Large trophy antlers often seen prominently displayed in grand houses and hotels can be found in auction and salerooms but a word of caution before buying; they are often too big for stickmaking, so don't be too envious when you look at these impressive specimens.

The surface and colour of antlers vary considerably, some are very rough to the touch while others are quite smooth and the colours range from very dark to pale, depending on where the animals graze. Dirty antlers can be cleaned with soap and water using a stiff brush, which can significantly change their appearance. An antler soaked for a few days in thin bleach will turn out to be almost white. When using bleach, it is advisable to remove as much of the pith from the horn as possible as it may cause severe discolouration.

Many people prefer the rough, dark-coloured antlers because they are more 'rustic' than some of the smoother, paler ones. However they can be uncomfortable to hold, especially for long periods of time. The roughness can be smoothed a little with files or abrasives without affecting the character too much, making the handle more comfortable to use, which is important in a working stick. Antler is a popular choice for many people who are eager to own a stick made from this natural material.

Other species

Reindeer and a few other species can be found in private herds, parks and zoos but obtaining their antlers is difficult. Antler imported from the Indian samba

Antlers from different breeds.

Various thicknesses of antler.

deer is regarded by many as the best because it has little or no pith, but it is difficult to obtain suitable pieces for stickmaking due to import restrictions.

Selecting antlers

When choosing an antler try to obtain one with a thick wall, so there is sufficient material available to enable it to be shaped onto the shank making a smooth joint. Thin-walled antlers often have insufficient material to make a good joint between the antler and shank. The shape and size of the antler you choose must match the shank so the result is a nicely balanced stick; avoid fitting a heavy antler onto a light shank or vice versa. The ideal thumb stick handle is one that can be used in either hand and in both forward and reverse directions, but because of the way antlers grow on the stags this desirable shape can be difficult to find. Perfectly acceptable thumb stick handles can be made from antlers that do not meet these criteria.

Safety with antlers

Antler points can be very sharp and should be removed from any handle as they may cause a serious injury if the user trips and falls onto the point.

Gamekeepers and rangers responsible for safety during planned shoots now ban antlers with sharp points because of the risk of injury.

Antler whistles

Do not throw away discarded antler tips as they make excellent whistles. The solid end prevents any air passing through the tip when blown; all the air is diverted past the reed and through the airway, which is essential when making a whistle.

To make a tip whistle, drill a $1\frac{1}{8}$in (30mm) deep x $\frac{1}{4}$in (6mm) diameter hole into the tip. Make a vertical cut $\frac{3}{16}$in (5mm) deep so it penetrates into the 6mm hole $\frac{1}{2}$in (12mm) from the front of the tip. Make an angled cut starting 12mm from the vertical cut until it meets with the bottom of the vertical cut to form the airway. Smooth off the sides of the airway. Make a 6mm diameter 15mm long dowel from wood, bone, antler or a plastic knitting needle to fit into the mouth of the whistle and file a flat side along the dowel about 2mm deep. The flat side can be made with a very gentle taper to divert the air against the shaped airway. Insert the dowel (reed) into the hole so it emerges at the front edge of the airway and test it to see if it whistles. Move the position of

the reed until it whistles. When a clear whistle is achieved, glue the reed in place and finish shaping the mouthpiece. The tone of the whistle will be quite shrill when using an antler tip, which makes them ideal for dog whistles.

Whistles can also be made on antler tines or the forks of thumb sticks providing the porous core (pith) at the bottom of the whistle hole is sealed to prevent the passage of air through it. A small amount of thin superglue dropped into the hole will seal the bottom, making it airtight.

Measurements for whistles can vary slightly depending on the size of the material available; changing the diameter and depth of the hole will change the sound of the whistle. It is well worth experimenting and practicing whistle-making on scrap pieces of antler or wooden shanks to gain experience before using a good antler.

If a whistle is fitted to an exhibition stick, ensure it works as judges will try it out; should it fail the stick will be downgraded.

An antler whistle.

MAKING ANTLER STICKS

Most antler sticks are made using the same basic method and techniques that are explained in the following steps. In order to avoid too much duplication, several different antlers are used to demonstrate the various procedures.

Step 1. Use antlers with substantial walls; very thin walled antlers can be used but they don't allow much room for dressing the antler to merge onto the shank. Before purchasing antlers, check the wall thickness. If buying from a remote dealer always request that antlers have substantial walls. Several different types of antlers are selected.

Step 2. Use a flat spade drill of the appropriate size to drill out the pith from the antler, drill a hole around $2^1/_2$in (65mm) deep. Most of the antlers featured were drilled using a 16mm drill.

A selection of antlers.

Antlers drilled for jointing.

Step 3. Choose a suitable shank to use with one of the drilled antlers. A dowel is made on the shank using a sharp knife, a junior hacksaw and a strip of abrasive cloth. Begin to make a dowel (peg) joint on the shank. Using a junior hacksaw, cut a shallow ring around the shank about $2^1/_2$in (65mm) from the end of the shank.

Step 4. Using a sharp knife, cut away surplus wood starting from the ring to the end of the shank to begin forming a dowel. Check frequently to ensure that not too much material is cut away.

Removing surplus wood from the dowel.

Step 5. With some wood removed, cut back towards the ring and form a sharp shoulder keeping the dowel as parallel as possible. When the dowel will almost fit into the hole drilled in the antler, use a strip of abrasive to round off the dowel until it is a tight fit. Check that the joint is close-fitting.

Step 6. Select an antler that will fit directly onto the shank without the need to fit a spacer in between the shank and antler. Dress the end of the antler so that

The dowel is complete.

A direct joint between antler and shank.

it makes a close-fitting joint between the dowel shoulder and the antler.

Fitting a spacer

Because antler shapes vary so much, finding an antler that perfectly matches with a shank can be difficult so an option regularly used by stickmakers is to fit a spacer between the antler and the shank.

Check the fit of the spacer ensuring that it will make a smooth transition between the antler and shank. If a single spacer will not complete a successful joint, consider using a thicker spacer or a combination of slim ones.

The thickness of spacers can vary considerably; thicker spacers are used when the antler shape is very uneven or irregular. Thicker spacers can be made from acrylics, bone, horn or wood, so always keep small offcuts from material cut from handle blanks or other projects. Pre-cut buffalo horn spacers and white camel bone spacers are popular and are available from some of the suppliers listed. Several thin spacers of different colours and materials can be used

Slip a spacer onto a dowel.

Check the fit of the spacer.

together to form an attractive joint between the handle and shank. A spacer has to be fitted with care, as there are several surfaces that have to be matched together to make clean and tight-fitting joints. Use some masking tape and wrap a couple of turns around the shank and antler, it will be used to mark the best position of the jointed sections. First ensure the spacer has two flat sides and maintain these flat surfaces at all times, test that the spacer fits tightly against the shoulder of the shank dowel, make any adjustments necessary on the shoulder. Mark the best position on the shank and on the spacer. Next ensure that the other side of the spacer fits tightly onto the base of the antler and again make any adjustments; make any adjustments on the antler and again mark the best position on the spacer and antler masking tape. The joint can be checked with all the marks aligned; if it is satisfactory, glue the joint together keeping all the marks lined up.

A method of checking joint alignment with thicker spacers.

FITTING CAPS

Caps can be fitted onto cut-off tines on thumb sticks and coronets to improve the look of the handle. If a spacer is used between the shank and handle, use the same material to make matching caps as together they help to improve the appearance of the handle.

Because caps are susceptible to knocks, they will often fall off if the joint is not reinforced. Caps simply glued onto antler are easily knocked off, especially if the stick accidently falls onto a hard surface. It is worth spending a little extra time to make the cap more secure. An effective method to improve the strength and effectiveness of a cap joint is described below.

Step 1. Using a flat file, carefully cut a perfectly flat surface on the antler and spacer so that a close-fitting joint is made between both surfaces.

A rust-proof screw inserted.

Step 2. Use a rust-proof countersunk screw, smear it with a little adhesive and screw into the middle of the pith, leaving the screw head to protrude about 3 to 4mm above the surface.

Step 3. Drill a hole in the cap to match the diameter and height of the screw head. Ensure that the cap fits closely onto the antler making a tight-fitting joint.

Cap drilled.

Step 4. Using a strong epoxy adhesive, glue the cap onto the antler ensuring that the flat surfaces are covered with adhesive and the hole in the cap is full of adhesive so it surrounds the counter-headed screw; secure the cap in place with tape until the adhesive has completely set. When the adhesive has set, remove the tape and check that the joint is both a neat fit and secure.

Cap held in place until glue has set.

Step 5. Using smooth files and abrasives, carefully merge the cap and handle together, remove any marks from the cap and antler and polish.

The completed cap.

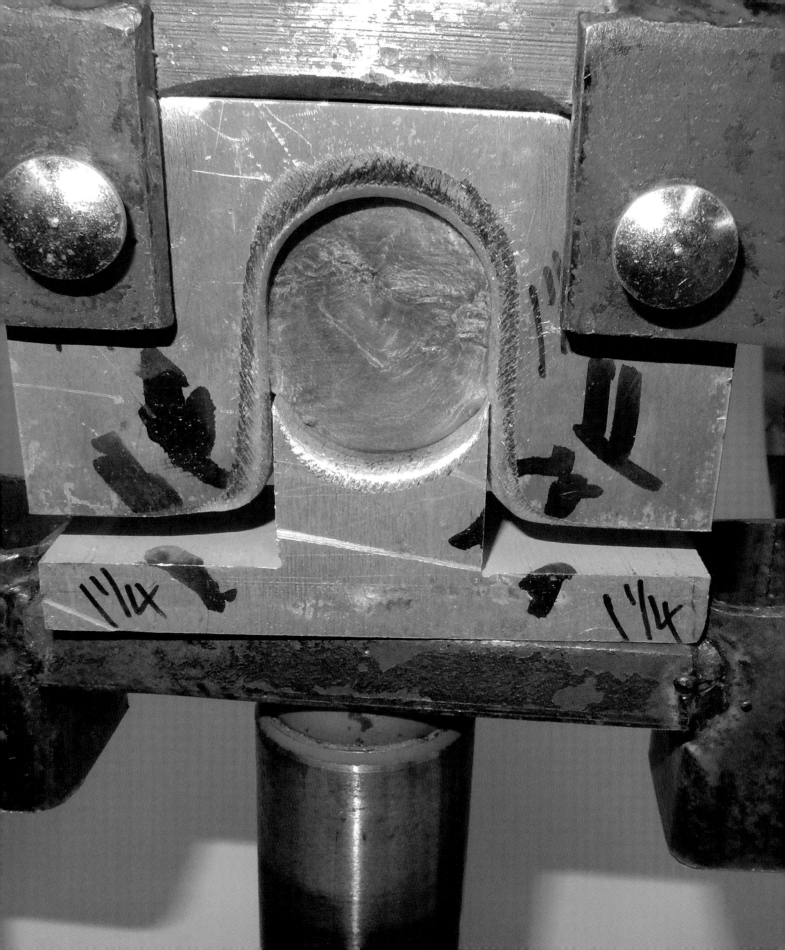

Chapter 10
Equipment for Working Horn

A substantial amount of specialist equipment is required if you intend to dress untreated or unrefined horns, especially when dressing cow and sheep horn. When the word 'specialist' is used it invariably means more expensive and difficult to obtain. The horns used for stickmaking fall into two principal categories; hollow or solid. A large proportion of cow, goat and sheep horns have a substantial hollow section, the part closest to the tip is solid horn. The hollow section of horn has to be squeezed (bulked) to make a solid horn that can then be shaped and dressed. Buffalo horn is normally supplied in a solid form with a gentle curve, whereas sheep's horn sometimes has severe curls that have to be removed to enable the horn to be dressed. Good-quality buffalo horn is usually supplied with fairly consistently shaped sides whereas sheep horns often have a convex and concave side that have to be squeezed into a more equal shape. A large proportion of cow horn is hollow and the walls are often quite thin, making them liable to collapse and fold when squeezed. Most goat horns are hollow and their walls are much lighter, causing them to collapse if squeezed, making them very difficult to dress satisfactorily. Occasionally, lighter horns can be

attached directly onto a shank without having to bulk or reshape the horn, making a useable stick. Because of the significant differences, buffalo horn requires considerably less equipment to shape it into a handle than the hollow sheep and cow horns. The amount of additional equipment and time required to dress cow and sheep horn is the primary reason why these handles are more difficult and expensive to make compared with buffalo horn. Another major factor is that good-quality sheep and cow horn is more difficult to obtain than buffalo horn, principally because farming methods for sheep and cattle have changed and legislation restrictions are more prohibitive than those for obtaining buffalo horn, even though the majority of it is imported.

The hollow horns have to be bulked to make them solid before they can be shaped and dressed into handles; specialized equipment is required to make the range of hollow and solid horn handles that are described below. The measurements shown are included for guidance only if anyone wishes to make their own equipment. The sizes of the equipment may be changed to suit individual preferences as required. It is

possible to make some of your own equipment such as formers and bulking blocks if you have the necessary skills and a suitably equipped workshop. Jigs and presses have to be strong enough to withstand substantial hydraulic pressures and they should be made by craftsmen with the appropriate level of skills and experience to ensure the equipment sufficiently robust. It is important to obtain well-made and strong presses as they are used with hydraulic jacks that produce tremendous pressures on all the components. Because some of this equipment is so specialized, it is generally only made to order by specialist fabricators. Second-hand equipment is sometimes offered for sale in the BSG magazine or on social media sites.

Hydraulic bottle jack

Hydraulic bottle jacks are used extensively for bulking and flattening horns in presses. They come in a range of sizes from 1 to 20 tons; the sizes used in the examples are mainly 10 and 12 tons. If stronger jacks are used, ensure that the presses will withstand the pressure generated by these more powerful jacks. A wide range of bottle

Left: A horn being bulked.

Hydraulic bottle jacks.

(12mm) thick and the four corner posts are 1in (25mm) diameter steel rod. Note that the top plate on the press has bowed slightly suggesting that a thicker plate should have been used, especially when using the most powerful jacks. The middle plate is allowed to float on top of the hydraulic jack so that it follows the profile of the horn but aligns the nose, crown and heel. Jubilee clips are attached to the corner posts to support the floating plate when the hydraulic bottle jack is removed for other duties. The jubilee clips are used so the height of the plate at rest can easily be altered.

Uncurling tool

This tool is used to remove the curls from horns, especially sheep's horns that often have severe curls. It is made from a piece of 24in (600mm) x 1in (25mm) square bar. The curved end bar is made from a piece of $1^5/_8$in (40mm) x $2^3/_4$in (60mm) x $1/_4$in (6mm) plate. The hook is made from a piece of steel $1^5/_8$ in (40mm) x 2in (50mm) x $1^1/_2$in (35mm). Larger or smaller tools can be made to suit a wide range of horns.

Universal press

This press is used for several jobs; removing concaves, tapering noses, straightening heels and bulking horns. In order to use this and other presses for multi-function tasks, the drilled holes in the presses and formers must be the same distance apart. The formers used in

Universal press, jack and concave block.

this press are drilled and tapped and are bolted to the top bar. When used to remove concave sections from a horn, a small steel flat plate is bolted onto the top rail of the press 4in (200mm) x 4in (200mm) x $1/_2$in (12mm) to provide a larger flat surface to push the horn against. When used as a heel press, the plate is removed and the heel press is bolted onto the top rail using the same two fixing holes. A set of cast aluminium bulking blocks can be bolted to the top rail when required, but are seldom used as newer and more specialized bulking blocks are used. The press is 18in tall x 10in wide. The base is 12in (300mm) x 6in (150mm) made from $5/_8$in (12mm) thick plate. The side and top bars are made from 2in (50mm) x 1in (25mm) steel bar and reinforced on each top

jacks are readily available from tool and garage suppliers.

Flattening press

The press is used to flatten and align most horn handles (buffalo, sheep, cow and goat) and is used in conjunction with a hydraulic bottle jack. The size of the featured press is 10in (250mm) x 10in (250mm) square x 18in (460mm) high. The three steel plates are $1/_2$in

Flattening press and jack.

Uncurling tool.

corner to reduce the risk of the bar bending when under pressure.

Heel blocks

Heel blocks are designed to straighten the heel of sheep and cow horn after it has been bulked; they can be used between the plates of a flattening press or fastened into the universal press. These blocks are subjected to a lot of pressure and they are best made from aluminium or steel – wooden blocks are liable to crack. A matching pair of heel blocks is bolted onto the press. The two sizes regularly used are 4in deep with a $1\frac{1}{4}$in diameter or $1\frac{1}{2}$in diameter hole.

Bulking press

The bulking press has been made to hold two different sets of bulking blocks and is a slightly different design to the universal and heel presses. The blocks are not drilled and tapped, the upper (female) block is held by a pair of loose-fitting bolts that allow some movement of the block so it can align with the lower (male) block. The bolts that hold the blocks in position are not subjected to any hydraulic pressure during the bulking process. The dimensions of the bulking press are 18in (460mm) tall x 12in (300mm) wide. The side supports are made from 2in (50mm) x 2in (50mm) steel square box section. Note; both side pillars have been extended by 3in (150mm) so the press can accommodate

A set of heel blocks.

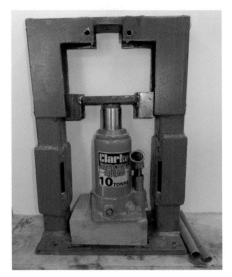

Bulking press.

some very large cow horns. Both the top corners have been reinforced with 'L' shaped steel plate so the top bar will withstand the pressure of a 12-ton hydraulic bottle jack. The press stands on a $\frac{1}{2}$in (12mm) base measuring 12in (300mm) x 6in (150mm). When bulking smaller horns, the jack stands on a block of timber to reduce the need for it to be extended so far. A removable carriage bar has been made to support and centralize the lower bulking blocks, which is quite helpful during the bulking process. Note that the height of the press has been extended to cope with large horns.

Bulking blocks (water cut)

This set of water-cut bulking blocks were cut using high pressure water, which results in more accurate cuts that help to prevent horn from being trapped between the surfaces of the male and female block. The overall size of each block is 4in (100mm) x $2\frac{3}{4}$in (70mm) deep. When the blocks are made, all the edges are very sharp and need to be rounded so that they don't cut into the

Water-cut bulking blocks.

horn during the bulking process. There are seven blocks in a set, starting with a $\frac{5}{8}$in (20mm) diameter hole rising in increments to $1\frac{1}{2}$in (40mm) in diameter.

Home-made bulking blocks

These blocks are hand-made from offcuts of aluminium, obtained from local scrap dealers who allow customers to salvage suitable pieces of aluminium from their skip. The aluminium is sold by weight, irrespective of the size and shape of the pieces. The measurements of these blocks vary; some are cut from 4in (100mm) x 4in (100mm) by $1\frac{5}{8}$in (40mm) thick aluminium, others are cut from 5in (130mm) x 3 in (80mm) x $1\frac{3}{4}$in (45mm) thick aluminium. The holes were drilled out in a professional workshop and range from $\frac{3}{4}$in (20mm) up to 2in (50mm) in diameter. The female section was cut out using a hacksaw, the cut-out piece made the male part, which was bolted onto a plate to prevent it from being forced too far into the female block and jamming under the hydraulic pressure. Files and rasps were used to remove all sharp corners which is both laborious and time consuming; these blocks were considerably less expensive than the water-cut blocks, but are not as accurate. Horn can get trapped between the sides during bulking which can tear the horn,

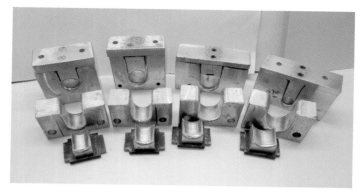

Home-made aluminium bulking blocks.

causing some damage. This has to be fixed in the later stages of dressing the horn. These blocks have been successfully used for many years to make numerous horn handles and are still used in conjunction with the newer water-cut blocks.

Hardwood bulking blocks can be used, providing the pressure is limited by using a much lower-rated hydraulic jack or a vice. There is a strong risk of wooden blocks splitting under pressure and subsequently they are not the recommended choice for bulking horns.

Concave removal blocks

The aluminium blocks shown were cast by an accomplished tradesman several years ago who had the necessary equipment to make the set. Cast aluminium blocks are very difficult to obtain as there are fewer people now making them.

Because of the shortage of aluminium blocks, most stickmakers use hardwood blocks for removing the concave from sheep horns. Hardwood blocks are not too difficult to make. Draw the outline

Aluminium concave removal blocks.

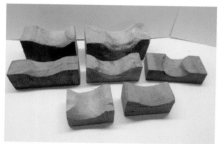

Home-made concave removal blocks.

curve of the horn onto a suitably sized block and cut a 'U' shape into the block with carving chisels or rotary cutters. Make a few blocks to cover all of the section of horn to be bulked. Keep the blocks for future use, and over time you will accumulate several blocks that will

suit a range of horns. The blocks are used in the universal press or the flattening press.

Bending jig

The bending jig is used to bend and shape all types of horn; buffalo, sheep, cow and goat. The jig is made from a piece of $1/4$in (6mm) thick steel plate measuring about 10in (250mm) square. A piece of 2in (50mm) angle iron is welded underneath the plate so the jig can be held in an engineering vice. On the left side of the jig a short section of angle iron approx. 4in (100mm) is fastened underneath the plate (it can be welded or secured using countersunk bolts). A pair of 10mm nuts are welded on the outside edge of the angle iron with holes through the angle iron allowing 10mm bolts to be screwed through the nuts which are used to hold the horn firmly onto the bending former. All the surface of the plate must be kept perfectly flat. Three pairs of holes are drilled in the plate at different distances from the angle iron on the left side to allow the bending formers to be repositioned, so larger diameter horns can be inserted and held between the bolts and the bending former. These

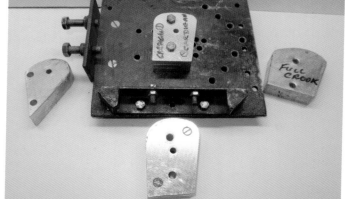

Bending jig and formers.

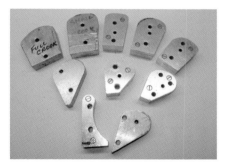

A collection of bending formers.

pairs of holes must correspond with the fixing holes in the shaping formers. A further series of 8mm holes are drilled around the bottom and right-hand side of the jig; these will provide a series of anchor points to hold clamps against when the horn is pulled around the former. Sections of angle iron are used as anchors and can be repositioned around the jig, providing all the holes are spaced accordingly.

Bending formers

Bending formers are used to shape all types of horn into a particular configuration. They can be made from several materials such as steel, aluminium, Tufnol or hardwood. The material should be a minimum of 1in (25mm) thick. The formers will be subjected to high temperatures during use. Metal formers are best as they will withstand the high temperatures better than timber and will last much longer, although they are more expensive and more difficult to cut to shape than timber. Timber formers can be made very quickly and cheaply if you own a jig or band saw and will last for several bending sessions. Tufnol will outlast timber, but is more expensive and it will eventually deteriorate when regularly subjected to high temperatures. If it is intended to make a lot of handles, aluminium is recommended as it will last indefinitely. The shape of the

formers is crucial as they must accurately replicate the inside line of a handle and if it is intended to make 'traditional' shaped handles such as crooks, cleeks, market and walking sticks, it is very important that the correct shape is used.

Nose-bending jig

A nose-bending jig is used to form a nose-out shape on all types of horn handles. Several types of horn handles have a turned-out nose, which can be troublesome to make. Some experienced stickmakers can successfully turn a nose using just a pair of 'mole grip' wrenches but it is much safer to use a bending jig, where you have more control over the horn. A nose-bending jig is not too difficult to make with a few appropriate engineering tools. The jig shown is 14in (360mm) x 12in (300mm) and $\frac{1}{4}$in (6mm) aluminium plate. A wooden base can be used if aluminium is unavailable; it may need to be made using thicker material than 6mm for strength. Use countersunk bolts to fasten a piece of angle iron or channel underneath the base so the jig can be fastened into a vice. Also using countersunk bolts, fasten another piece of angle iron under the top edge of the base plate which is used to clamp the neck of the horn handle into position. Using a template or a handle with a turned-out nose, place the neck section flush against the angle iron; this will enable you to mark

where the inside bend of the nose appears on the jig. Drill a cluster of 12mm holes around the area, which can be used for different-sized handles. A strong pin such as a 12mm diameter bolt is fixed into the most appropriate hole and the nose is carefully and slowly pulled around the bolt using a sash clamp. The last job is to drill a series of holes around the edge of the base plate forming a semi-circle. Strong bolts are fixed into these holes and are the anchor points to which a sash clamp is attached, to pull the horn around the pin.

Sash clamp

A 24in (600mm) long sash clamp is the ideal tool for use with the nose-bending jig because of its length. The older style of clamps seem to work better than the modern versions and can often be found at car boot sales or second-hand tool dealers. Another advantage of these clamps is that the head doesn't turn against the horn when in use.

Nose-tapering jig

Often when making a nose-out handle using horn, there is too much material to turn satisfactorily. Tapering the nose section to be turned makes it easier to shape the horn and it also improves the appearance of the nose. A simple jig can be made from a piece of 1in square steel

Nose-bending jig.

Nose-tapering jig.

box section by cutting off one side and welding the cut-off piece to form a taper within the three-sided box. A tapered wedge can also be used within the cut-off box section to increase the taper if required. The jig is used in either the flattening or universal press.

Round-tapered punch

A selection of different diameters of round-tapered steel or brass punches is useful when bulking horns. They are inserted into the hollow section of the horn, which is squeezed onto the punch preventing the horn from collapsing. These can be used in conjunction with tapered wooden pegs. The tapered punch is slowly withdrawn from the horn as it is squeezed onto the punch and the squashed wooden peg remains in the horn; it can be drilled out as bulking process proceeds.

Wedges

A selection of metal (brass, copper, steel and so on) or wooden wedges is useful for aligning horns during flattening and shaping procedures. They are placed under or on top of a horn so that the crown, heel and nose are brought into line with the neck while the horn is being flattened or shaped.

Clamps

A varied selection of good-quality strong clamps is essential for pulling horns into shape around formers. Some of the clamps featured are the 'piston' type, which are good for pulling horns as the piston does not turn when in use. Most clamps turn the head when in use, causing it to slip off the horn. A deep-throated 'G' clamp is useful for holding a horn onto the base plate during the bending process.

Tapered steel punches.

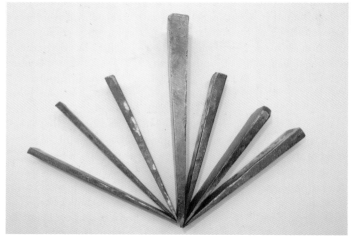

Steel and brass wedges.

Various clamps.

Water receptacles

Most horns need to be boiled at the start of the shaping and dressing procedure and a suitably sized receptacle is required to contain the horn; various options are available. An electrical urn is a popular choice as they are large enough to hold most sizes. Several horns can be boiled at once, which is useful when uncurling sheep's horn in session. Large saucepans can be used for medium-sized horns.

A large oval jam pan used in conjunction with a gas burner is a good option, as it is large enough to hold and submerse the horn(s) in boiling water. Take care when using a naked flame within a workshop environment; it is safer to use a naked flame outdoors.

A large pan.

Jam pan.

Electric hot air gun

Electric hot air guns are used extensively in shaping all types of horn. They are rated from 1,200 watts up to around 2KW and are readily available from most DIY shops. The heat output can be varied on some models, which is useful when only a limited amount of heat is required. They will burn horns if they are left in the same position for long periods so care has to be taken when using these machines. Keep them away from any flammable materials.

Electric hot air guns.

Press for bending heavy horns

The design of this bending press allows horns to be pushed between a pair of rollers. The distance between the rollers can be varied, as can the diameter of the rollers. The diameter of the round bar used to push the horn between the rollers can also be changed. These variable adjustments allow the press to be used to produce a range of shapes. With a strong hydraulic bottle jack, large heavy horns can easily be bent using this jig. Take care with this press as horns can be quickly bent too far.

Gas torches

Gas torches have many uses; they are used extensively in the building, plumbing and decorating trades and are a most useful appliance to have. Gas torches are very useful for heating specific sections of horns when used

Press for bending heavy horns.

Gas torches.

with a small flame. There are several types of gas burners and torches available; some operate using gas cylinders with a flexible hose and ranges of nozzles are available from very fine to large. For occasional use, torches are available that operate from small gas canisters often used by campers. The small nozzles produce a fine flame that can be used carefully to heat sections of horn, such as a nose or a concave section of a sheep's horn.

Chapter 11
Making Buffalo Horn Handles

Most buffalo horn is imported from India and China and yet it is easier to obtain than British-reared sheep's horn. The solid tips of buffalo horn are used for stickmaking and they are available in lengths from a few inches up to and exceeding 18in (460mm), which is more than sufficient to make a full decorated crook, making them a popular choice with stickmakers. The principal importer is advising that the longer horns are getting more difficult to obtain and are therefore more expensive, as fewer older buffalo (like sheep) that grow longer horns are being kept by farmers.

Short, heavy sections of buffalo horn can be obtained which are suitable for making cardigan, thumb sticks or half-head handles. Pieces of machined horn can be purchased in a variety of round and flat sections, which are very useful for stickmakers as they can be used for caps, spacers and ferrules. Several styles of pre-shaped handles are also available in buffalo horn from some of the suppliers listed.

Coloured buffalo horn

Generally, most of the buffalo horn supplied for stickmaking is black; occasionally horns will have some streaks of colour running within the horn, giving a stick handle much more character. Full coloured horns become available once in a while; they are extremely rare and expensive but they make stunning handles. If the opportunity ever arises to obtain a full coloured horn, take it – you may never get another chance. Apparently coloured horns are often bought by clothing manufacturers, who use them to make buttons and other accessories on exclusive and fashionable clothes.

Selecting horn

Over many decades of working horns, stickmakers have improved the technique of shaping and dressing buffalo horn. Today we can apply their knowledge and experience with modern technology to manipulate the horn with much less difficulty than previously encountered. As a result, buffalo horn has become a popular medium for making quality handles on a range of sticks and is now available from many sources and suppliers, making selection an important factor as some horns offered for sale are unsuitable for making good-quality handles.

A lot of buffalo horn is purchased from online sites and selecting the most suitable horn can be a little uncertain, therefore choose a reputable supplier who will listen to your requirements and will endeavour to supply you with a product that meets your specifications. Some suppliers grade horns into three groups; 'A' being premium, 'B' medium and 'C' being low quality. Premium quality horns should be free from any defects or flaws and be suitable to make the highest quality handles; B-grade horns are a lower quality and may have some imperfections but are suitable to make decent working stick handles. C-rated (craft rated) horns are low quality and are normally only suitable for making bits and pieces of handles such as spacers, collars and tips or for other craftwork.

Select a horn of sufficient width and length to make your chosen handle. The width of a horn is just as important as the length. Take care when choosing lower-graded horns as the width can vary considerably along the length and may contain sections that are too thin to make an acceptable handle.

Horn sizes

The following list gives the minimum length of horn required to make a particular style of handle. It is sensible to buy longer pieces, as the tip may be damaged or unsuitable. A ladies' nose-in walking stick handle will require a horn of 12in (305mm). A nose-in market stick handle will require a horn of 13in (330mm). A nose-out market stick will require a horn of 15in (380mm). A plain full crook will require a horn in excess of 16in (410mm). Thicker and longer horns may be required if it is intended to carve an object; consider reversing a heavy horn and use the tip as the neck and the base for carving an object on the nose.

Pre-shaped buffalo horns

A comprehensive range of pre-shaped buffalo horns are available from some of the stickmaking suppliers listed. Some of the handles available range from knob sticks, thumb sticks, riding crops, pony foot, crook, market and walking stick handles that only need a small amount of work to finish them to an acceptable standard. Some of the horns simply need to be polished and fitted onto a shank; others are available with sufficient material to turn your own nose. These pre-shaped horns mitigate the need to obtain much of the equipment required to work a 'raw' horn and are an excellent choice for anyone with limited workshop space, equipment and tools. Some of the horns can be altered and adjusted to change their shape and appearance quite easily when using some of the formers and jigs described above. Please be aware that you should not enter pre-shaped handles in most stickmaking competitions, as often the rules require that a stick must be completely made by the competitor. Experienced judges can identify some of the most common pre-shaped handles and they will often place these at the back of the rack without making any comment, to avoid a conflict with the contestant. Check the competition rules before entering.

Pre-shaped sheep and cow horns

Unlike the pre-shaped buffalo horns, pre-shaped sheep and cow horn handles are seldom available; some stickmakers may make a one-off handle from sheep or cow horn when requested. Generally, stickmakers prefer to make a complete stick as it is usually uneconomical to make just a handle. A lot of people expect to obtain a sheep or cow handle for a similar price as a buffalo horn and in some cases as a wooden handle, as they have no idea as to the amount of time, equipment and effort that is required to make a handle. It is not a viable option to provide a dressed sheep or cow horn for the price most people are willing to pay.

Tools and equipment

The presses, clamps, jigs and formers described in the previous chapter are used to form and shape the horns. Some specific tools are introduced in the step-by-step guides and it is recommended that good-quality tools are used, as buffalo horn is a hard and demanding material requiring premier quality equipment. Engineering tools are more suitable than woodworking equipment as they are designed to deal with harder materials. Good-quality engineering tools such as drills and files will cope easily with buffalo and other horn.

Heating the horn

Buffalo horn has to be heated in order to bend and shape it. There are two methods of heating horn regularly used; immersing the horn in boiling water and heating the horn using an electric hot air gun. Gas torches can be used with great care.

Boiling horn

Before trying to bend a horn it is placed in boiling water for a period of thirty to forty minutes, depending on the size of the horn. Heating the horn in boiling water does not burn it and the heat penetrates into the core, allowing it to be bent more easily. The heat is maintained during the bending and shaping process using a hot air gun. The horn will not be damaged if it is left in boiling water for a longer period.

Dry heat

If it is not possible to boil the horn, it can be heated using an electric hot air gun or a gas torch. The main risk with heating the horn using either method is burning the surface. The heat must be allowed sufficient time to penetrate into the core of the horn without burning the surface. It is advisable to 'rest' the heating for short periods to allow the horn time to absorb the heat. Electric hot air guns are mostly used; the best ones have variable heat control, which is beneficial especially when turning noses. Hot air guns are available from most DIY and hardware shops for around £30.

Gas torches and the older-fashioned paraffin blowlamps can be used with care to heat buffalo horns, but they are seldom used because the severity of the heat they generate can quickly burn the exterior. Gas torches with small nozzles are useful to direct a gentle flame onto a specific area when a small section of horn has to be moved, such as turning a nose or removing a concave from a ram's horn. Wrapping horns with aluminium baking foil will reduce the risk of scorching, but great care must be taken when using excessive dry heat. When using any form of dry heat, allow sufficient time for it to penetrate to the core of the horn.

TURNING A NOSE ON PRE-SHAPED BUFFALO HORNS

Pre-shaped buffalo handles can be obtained from some of the suppliers with sufficient length to turn out a nose. A club member bought a pair of these horns and asked if I would turn out a nose on each of the handles, as he didn't have any suitable equipment. The following procedure was used to turn the noses on each of the buffalo horn handles, which should be helpful for anyone wishing to use these pre-shaped horns. Both horns were good quality and the crowns had been bent to an acceptable shape with sufficient length left to turn out a nose.

A nose-bending jig, a 24in sash clamp and a hot air gun are used for turning a nose on any type of horn. A selection of wedges is useful to help in maintaining the alignment during the bending process. Because the nose section of a horn is relatively small, it can be heated sufficiently with an electric hot air gun. It is most important not to overheat the horn or it will crack, just apply sufficient heat to turn it and concentrate the heat on the inside line of the bend throughout the procedure.

Step 1. Mark the position of the bend on the horn, ensuring that the base of the turned nose will be about $1/2$in (12mm) above the base of the heel. Make an allowance for the thickness of the horn in your measurements when it is turned around the bending pin; it is essential that the base of the nose sits above the base of the heel to maintain a nicely shaped handle.

Step 2. Using the mark, position the horn on the jig so the inside point of the bend sits tightly against the bending pin, adjust the position of the horn or bending pin as necessary. Securely fasten and clamp the horn (heel and

Clamp the horn in position to turn the nose.

crown) in place so it cannot move during the nose-bending procedure. Place the sash clamp in a position so the first bend of the nose can be pulled part way around the bending pin, tighten the clamp but do not attempt to move the horn.

Step 3. Heat the horn with a hot air gun, ensuring the inside is heated as close to the point of the bend as possible. Use a steel ruler or a flat piece of steel to deflect the heat specifically onto the inside of the section to be bent. It is important to concentrate the heat on the inside line of the nose. Carefully tighten the clamp while maintaining the heat until the horn begins to move; stop the heat as soon as the horn moves – do not overheat or it will crack.

Step 4. Allow the bent section of horn to

Begin to turn the nose.

Reposition the horn to tighten the nose.

cool a little until it is stable. When the horn has stabilized, reposition the sash clamp on the jig so the horn can be pulled further around the pin. Heat the horn, again on the inside of the bend, at the point of the bend keeping the horn tightly against the bending pin and carefully apply pressure using the sash clamp. Check that the nose is maintaining a parallel line with the handle; if it moves out of line adjust it while there is sufficient heat in the horn using clamps or wedges. The horn shape may change while turning the nose, therefore place the horn onto a bending jig and re-adjust the shape of the handle and nose while it is held against the former.

Step 5. Allow the horn to cool and when stable, release it from the jig.

Nose turned around bending pin.

A pair of turned noses.

Step 6. A bulge will often form on both sides of the bend, which is normal on a large horn. Dress the horn; remove the bulges and tidy up the inside of the bend. The final dressing is completed when the handle is fastened onto a shank. Both the pre-shaped horn noses were turned using this method.

The jig, clamps and method of turning these noses are used on both sheep and cow horn.

Cutting the horn

Very large buffalo horns need to have surplus material removed before boiling and shaping them to reduce the thickness, to make the bending process easier. Before cutting off surplus material, give some thought as to the final shape of the handle you require as removing horn incorrectly will make it difficult to obtain your chosen shape. If it is intended to make a handle with a square heel, it is advisable to cut the horn with a shallow step in the outside edge about 3in from the base, which will help to form the heel. If a round heel is required, cut the horn with parallel sides.

If a horn is simply cut with parallel edges, it will tend to form a round heel rather than one with a square heel. I obtained a number of buffalo horns that had been cut with parallel sides, limiting their potential; it is likely that they will only make round-heeled handles.

Cutting horn for square and round heels.

MAKING A PRESENTATION STICK WITH A COLLAR

The steps taken in making this handle and stick can be used when making most types of horn-handled sticks. Some of the later guides may not contain the amount of detail covered here but most of these steps are necessary to make an acceptable stick with a collar. Including all the steps in this guide will avoid too much duplication and repetition in later guides.

I received a request to make a presentation stick for a keen walker who was retiring from a financial company. His colleagues ordered a nose-in buffalo handle with a round heel and an engraved silver collar fitted between the shank and handle. The request for a round handle enabled me to use a horn that had been cut with parallel sides. A horn was selected with sufficient length and thickness for the handle; there was sufficient horn to use a collar with a 25mm outside diameter. In this sequence, several steps have been included for heating and shaping a nose-in handle, straightening a shank, fitting a silver collar, fitting a ferrule and dressing and finishing the horn and shank.

Step 1. Select a suitably sized horn, bearing in mind the desired length, shape and size of the handle. The horn used for the handle is 12in long and has sufficient diameter to make a market-style handle that will fit with a silver collar with an outside diameter of 25mm. An engraved silver collar was ordered.

Step 2. Prepare a container and begin boiling sufficient water to cover the first section of the horn to be bent (ideally the whole horn is best submersed). Prepare a suitable former to shape the horn and have a range of clamps and

Use a parallel cut horn.

equipment ready. Boil the horn for around thirty minutes before removing it with a pair of tongs or gloves.

Boil the horn for thirty to forty minutes.

Step 3. Clamp the hot horn firmly onto the bending jig, ensuring the horn is kept flat onto the surface of the jig throughout the shaping process. With the heel of the horn clamped firmly in place, begin pulling the first bend around the former using a strong clamp. It is advisable to insert a piece of non-slip abrasive between the clamp and horn to prevent the clamp from slipping off. When the first section is bent, hold it in place so it cannot move using another clamp, before releasing the first clamp from the horn. It is vital that the hot horn is held securely in place and is not allowed to move during all the bending sequences. Use an electric hot air gun to maintain the temperature on the inside

line of the horn before bending the next section.

Step 4. Pull the next section of horn tightly onto the former and clamp it tightly in position; remove the first clamp when the horn is held securely by a second clamp. Maintain the temperature on the inside line of the horn using a hot air gun during all the bending sequences. On longer horns such as crooks, these sequences may be repeated several times to shape a horn completely around a former.

Step 5. Because of the short length of the horn and shape of the handle, the next stage of the bending process requires the horn to be transferred onto another jig to form the rounded nose. Allow the horn to cool and set before removing or loosening any clamps. If clamps are loosened while the horn is

Pulling the second bend around the former.

warm, there is a risk that the horn will try to revert to its original shape and crack on the inside line.

Step 6. Transfer the cooled horn onto a circular former and firmly fasten it in place to prevent any unwanted movement. Using a hot air gun, concentrate the heat on the inside of the section of nose to be bent. Pull the heated nose section around the circular former to make a smooth, curved nose and allow the horn to fully cool before releasing any clamps.

Step 7. When the horn has cooled, remove it from the jig and begin dressing it using a range of rasps and files until the desired shape is achieved. Concentrate on the shape of the inside line first; when the inside shape is correct, use it as a guide to shape the outside line and the sides of the handle.

Pulling the first bend around the former.

Pull in the nose on a circular jig.

Dress the horn to shape.

Gradually reduce the overall size of the horn until it is an appropriate shape and size to make a handle and fit into a 25mm diameter collar.

Step 8. A threaded rod is used to join the handle onto the shank. An 8mm hole is drilled to a depth of about 2 in (65mm) into the centre of the base of the horn handle and a length of 8mm diameter threaded rod is glued in using an epoxy adhesive.

When the glue has fully set, a 25mm diameter washer can be fastened against the base of the horn using a tightened nut; the washer makes an ideal guide to form the base of the handle, which is dressed evenly to almost the diameter of the washer. The remaining horn is dressed accordingly.

Threaded rod glued into the horn.

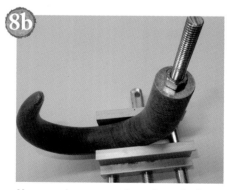

Use a washer as a guide to dress the horn.

Begin fitting a collar onto the handle.

Dress the handle ready for fitting to the shank.

Step 9. With the horn dressed down to almost the diameter of the 25mm steel washer, a rebate has to be cut onto the base to allow the horn to fit inside the silver collar. The diameter of the rebate section is 23mm. Use a small hacksaw to cut a circle around the base of the horn, a distance of half the length of the collar from the base, ensuring that a perfect circular ring is formed around the horn. Very carefully file away surplus horn until the rebated horn fits perfectly inside the collar; ensure that the collar fits tightly against the wall of the rebate cut into the horn. Rather than using the sterling silver collar in case it is damaged, it is advisable to use an identical-sized nickel collar as a template to dress the horn until it fits perfectly.

Step 10. When the rebate fits perfectly inside the collar, complete dressing the horn so it matches exactly with the external diameter of the collar. Begin with a fairly coarse grit abrasive (100 grit) to remove any file marks or deep scratches from the horn. An alternative method of removing scratches is to use cabinet scrapers – they are ideal for removing scratches and file marks from most of the materials used for handles. Carefully draw the scraper along the horn following the grain direction, which will remove very fine layers. A range of different shaped cabinet scrapers are available to cope with curved and flat surfaces. Continue the final dressing, reducing the grit size with each pass of abrasives until a fine grit size of around 400 to 600 grit is used. Continue dressing the horn using fine 0000 grade wire wool in conjunction with a paste abrasive such as T-Cut until all scratches and marks are removed from the horn. Complete dressing the handle by buffing and polishing using a rotary polishing machine with two types of buffing blocks. Using the polishing machine will highlight any marks or scratches that remain; these can be removed during the final stages of dressing the horn when it is fitted onto the shank.

Step 11. Select a suitable shank of the correct diameter to fit perfectly with the 25mm diameter collar. The length of the shank required is around 44in (1,120mm) giving a total length of around 48in (1,220mm) for the whole stick. It is well worth having several different diameter shanks available when using collars as a decoration, as it can be quite difficult to find a shank with the exact diameter of a collar.

Step 12. Straighten the selected shank and cut it at a point where the diameter matches the external diameter of the collar. Using the same method as used

Handle ready for fitting onto the shank.

Step 14. With the stick fully assembled, complete the finishing process. Remove any traces of surplus adhesive from the joints and remove any remaining scratches or marks from the handle, dress the shank removing any flaking bark and dress any protrusions caused by tiny offshoots. When completely satisfied apply several coats of your preferred finish to the shank and handle, allowing plenty of time between coats for the finish to dry and cure. Some stickmakers use a microcrystalline wax polish as a final finish, which can be over-coated as required by the owner.

The finished presentation stick.

on the horn, cut a shallow rebate on the shank that will fit tightly inside the collar. The combined length of the rebate on the shank and the horn handle needs to be slightly less than the overall length of the collar, so the shank and collar will have a tiny gap between them for the adhesive. Check that the shank, collar and handle make a perfect fitting joint and that the handle and shank are aligned before gluing all the components together.

Step 13. Cut the shank to length and cut a rebate to suit a ferrule; the rebate may be tapered or almost parallel depending on the style of ferrule used. Glue the ferrule onto the shank using epoxy, ensuring it fits up to the shoulder of the rebate.

MAKING A BUFFALO CROOK HANDLE

In order to make a full crook handle with a turned-out nose, a buffalo horn of at least 16in (410mm) long is required. The horn needs to have an even and consistent thickness along its length that tapers gently towards the tip, which will allow a suitable shaped nose to be made on the crook. A horn of this length will have a large base that can be reduced in size before the bending and shaping procedure begins; removing surplus horn must be done carefully in order to make a square heel on the crook. Avoid horns with a severe undulating surface and a deep concave along one side, as they are difficult to remove or deal with during the later dressing sequence. It is not necessary to buy a very heavy or thick horn, as the finished crook will not exceed $1\frac{1}{4}$in (30mm) in diameter along its length; however, ensure that there is sufficient width and depth to make a well-shaped and proportioned crook handle. Some buffalo horns have natural bumps and hollows which make them unsuitable for making a crook. A solid horn with a smooth surface and a gradual reduction in size from the base to nose is the best choice to make a nicely shaped crook handle.

Buffalo horns of the size needed to make a full crook are very strong and they make excellent handles for working sticks, due to their strength and appearance when finished. Because of their hardness, they are quite difficult to shape and require a selection of strong clamps, a strong jig, an accurate former and good-quality tools and equipment. Take time to have the appropriate tools and equipment at hand before commencing the bending and shaping process. This will include a bending jig and former, a hot air gun, a range of clamps and wedges and some non-slip abrasive blocks.

Step 1. Mark out the horn so that a square heel will be formed. Cut off all surplus horn and remove any sharp edges before submersing in the hot water. Sharp edges can encourage the beginning of a crack or tear to appear in the horn during the bending process, so need to be removed.

Horns cut to form a square heel.

Step 2. Allow the horn to boil in the water for around thirty to forty minutes in a suitable container. Note that an oval jam pan is used to heat the longer horns.

Boil the horn for thirty to forty minutes.

Step 3. While the horn is in the water, set out your tools and equipment in readiness to shape the horn on your workbench. Using tongs or gloves

remove the horn from the hot water and fasten it firmly onto your shaping jig. Ensure it is securely held onto the flat surface of the jig base plate.

Horn clamped onto a bending jig.

Step 4. Position the first clamp onto the jig so it will pull the first bend of the horn tightly onto the former. It will be necessary to maintain the heat in the area of the horn to be bent using a hot air gun. Always concentrate the heat on the inside section of the bend; do not overheat the horn as it can cause it to crack. Pull the first bend and maintain the pressure at all times. Use another clamp to hold the horn before removing the first clamp. It is crucial throughout the bending sequence that a hot horn is held firmly in place until it cools and sets; if a warm horn is allowed to open it is likely to crack.

Pull the first bend and secure the horn

Step 5. Heat the next section to be bent, concentrating the heat along the inside line of the horn. When the horn is up to temperature, pull the next bend onto the former with a strong clamp. It may be necessary to use a non-skid block to prevent the clamp from slipping off the horn. When the bend is tightly against the former use another clamp to hold the horn in place, allowing the clamp to be removed or repositioned. Throughout the shaping process, ensure the crown section of the horn is held flat onto the base plate of the jig to keep the nose and heel sections aligned. Allow the horn to cool completely before removing it from the jig.

Pull the horn around the former.

Step 6. The nose is turned using the same jigs and procedure as used earlier.

Turning the nose.

Step 7. Begin dressing the horn using rasps, files and abrasives to achieve a smooth finish. Cabinet scrapers can be used successfully on buffalo horn to remove any file marks or scratches. Use wire wool with a liquid abrasive; it will show any file marks or scratches made on the horn.

Before completing the handle it may be necessary to alter the overall shape of the horn following the nose-turning sequence to obtain the desired crook shape. If so clamp the horn onto a jig and former, concentrate the heat on the sections to be reshaped using a hot air gun and use clamps to pull it into position on the former. Allow the horn to cool before removing it from the former and commence dressing it using rasps and files until a suitable surface is achieved.

Continue dressing the horn leaving a little spare material until the final dressing is completed, when the shank is fitted on.

Step 8. Select a shank that complements the handle; the diameter of the shank at the handle joint should be around 1in (25mm) reducing slightly towards the tip to around $\frac{7}{8}$in (22mm). Use a washer as a template and mark the most suitable position to drill an 8mm diameter hole on the base of the horn. The position should suit both the horn and shank; it may not necessarily be exactly in the centre of the horn.

Step 9. Drill an 8mm hole into the horn to a depth of about $2\frac{1}{2}$in (65mm). Mark the position to drill a hole in the shank and drill an 8mm diameter hole of $2\frac{1}{2}$in (65mm). Use a 5in length of 8mm studding as a template and locate the position where the handle and shank make a perfect joint. Use masking tape on the horn and shank to mark the best position. When completely satisfied that the joint is perfect and handle and

Start dressing the horn.

Re-shape the horn if necessary.

Continue dressing the horn.

Hold the joint in position until glue sets.

shank are aligned, mark the position on the masking tape. Glue the joint together using epoxy adhesive and check that the fit and alignment are perfect; maintain pressure on the joint until the glue sets.

Step 10. When the glue has completely set, begin to dress the handle so that it merges with the shank making a perfect joint. Use fine files to avoid making deep marks in the horn, continue dressing the complete handle until a satisfactory overall shape is achieved throughout the whole crook. Use abrasives in sequence until a smooth finish is achieved without any scratch or file marks showing. A cabinet scraper can be used to make a smooth, scratch-free surface.

Step 11. Polish the horn. A rotary polishing machine will save time and make an excellent finish. Polishing

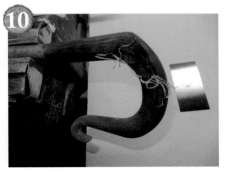

Merge the handle onto the shank.

Finish the shank and complete the stick.

Some finished buffalo-handled sticks.

MAKING A BLACK SWAN

A buffalo horn swan neck is difficult to shape using the normal bending jigs and formers, so it was decided to use a bending jig designed to bend large horns. The strong jig has a pair of rollers that can be spaced at different distances to cope with various sizes of horn. A section of steel round bar is used in conjunction with a hydraulic jack to push the horn up and between the pair of rollers. By using different sizes of round bar or pipe and adjusting the distance between the rollers, several shapes can be made using this jig and even the largest horns can be bent using a powerful hydraulic jack.

Step 1. Select a large horn with sufficient length and width to form the neck and head. Place it into boiling water for around forty minutes to soften. Set up the distance between the rollers in the bending jig to suit the size of the horn and the shape required.

Step 2. Place the hot horn in between the pair of rollers; the horn for a swan neck is pushed upwards between the rollers using a 12-ton hydraulic jack, which forms the curved neck. Allow the horn to cool and set in its new shape before removing it from the jig.

machines are a worthwhile investment if you intend to make several horn-handled sticks. Buffing and polishing mops can be attached to electric drills if a polishing machine is unavailable.

Step 12. Fit a ferrule onto the tip of the shank. Smooth off any protrusions and remove any loose bark. Using a fine abrasive to smooth the whole shank and remove any dust with a clean cloth.

Apply sanding sealer to the shank; additional coats may be applied as required. When the sealer has completely dried, apply several coats of your preferred finish. Allow the finish to dry and harden before finally polishing the whole stick with a good-quality wax polish.

Using the methods described, several types of buffalo-handled sticks can be made.

Horn bent into the shape of a swan neck.

Step 3. Remove any surplus horn from the head section and carefully begin forming the swan's head and beak. The horn requires a considerable amount of work to dress the head and neck of the swan. Eventually the outline of the swan's head begins to emerge from the horn.

The head shape beginning to emerge.

Step 4. Continue dressing the horn and start to form the detail of the head and beak. Insert the eye sockets and refine the neck section of the swan until an acceptable shape is achieved.

Step 5. Make a rebate on the horn and shank to fit a silver or nickel collar between the handle and the shank. The collar will help to enhance the black handle against the shank.

Head, beak and eyes detailed.

Cut a rebate on the horn for a collar.

Step 6. Attach the handle to the shank, ensuring that the collar is a neat fit. Colour the beak, fit the eyes, complete dressing the handle and remove all marks and scratches from the horn. Smooth off any protrusions from the shank, seal and finish the shank with a product of your choice. Fit a ferrule. Polish the handle using rotary mops until an acceptable finish is achieved. Protect the handle using a wax polish to maintain the finish.

The completed swan.

MAKING A HEAVY HIKING STICK

A request to make a specific type and size of stick was received by a gentleman who frequently led groups of walkers along tracks and paths in and around the Lake District. The handle had to be a nose-in black buffalo horn, a tall, heavy, dark shank with a spike was required that would withstand the rough terrain. A silver rolled collar had to be fitted between the handle and shank. The height of the stick and the approximate size of the handle were received from the customer. The following steps briefly describe how the stick was made.

Step 1. A heavy horn was selected that would make a large nose-in handle. The horn was immersed in boiling water for about forty minutes and then firmly clamped onto a bending jig with a former attached.

Step 2. Maintain heat in the large horn using a hot air gun and begin pulling the horn onto the former. Abrasive cloth is used between the horn and clamp, which reduces the chance of the clamp slipping off the horn during the bending process.

Step 3. Reheat the horn and continue pulling it around the former. Use a hot air gun to maintain the heat along the inside line of the horn during the bending sequence. The surplus tip was cut off the nose section of the horn, which was allowed to cool.

Step 4. In order to improve the shape of the nose-in handle, it was transferred onto a circular bending jig. The nose section of the horn was reheated using a hot air gun, again concentrating the heat on the inside line. The horn was pulled into shape around a circular jig.

Step 5. The horn is allowed to completely cool before releasing any clamps to prevent the horn from moving. Remove the horn, which is now ready to begin the dressing process.

Step 6. Begin to dress the horn using rasps and files. Avoid using coarse files that will cause deep marks as the final shape is reached. Cut in a rebate to suit a rolled collar that will be fitted between the handle and shank.

Step 7. Ensure that the rolled collar is a neat and tight fit on the handle, making any adjustments that are necessary.

Step 8. Use a length of 8mm threaded rod to form the joint. Complete dressing the handle and glue the collar onto the handle. Make a rebate on the shank to suit the collar, again ensuring that it is a neat fit. Assemble the joint and collar and glue together ensuring all parts are aligned and close fitting.

Step 9. Fit an alpine spike on the tip of the shank. A long, tight-fitting taper is required on the shank to make a strong joint between the spike and shank. Glue the spike in place, ensuring that all the wood is covered in glue to help protect it against wet conditions. Finally, pin the spike in position for added strength and security.

Step 10. Polish the handle and apply a finish to the shank. In this instance, the customer requested that linseed oil was to be used on the shank.

The horn clamped on a bending jig.

Begin bending the horn.

The horn pulled around the former.

Pulling the horn around circular former.

The shaped horn ready for dressing.

Dressing the horn and cutting a rebate.

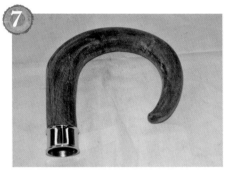

Rolled collar tested on the handle.

The joint completed.

The alpine spike fitted and pinned.

The completed stick.

Chapter 12
Making Sheep and Cow Horn Handles

Good-quality sheep and cow horns are difficult to obtain, chiefly due to modern farming methods and regulations imposed on farmers and abattoirs regarding the movement and control of animals and their parts. Many animals are 'de-horned' at an early age and some modern breeds do not grow horns. However, limited supplies of both sheep and cow horns are available from some of the suppliers listed; there are also several dealers on internet sites that sell horns. It is best to see and examine the horns before buying, otherwise use a supplier that has been recommended by regular users as a lot of inferior horns are sold that are unsuitable for stickmaking, although they may be suitable for other craftwork.

The cost of top-quality horns suitable for stickmaking continues to increase because of the limited availability. Rather like shanks, horns need to season for at least a year before use. Newly cut horns will try to revert to their original shape if they are used too soon; allow at least a year before bulking and shaping horns, if time permits allow the horns a longer time to cure before using them.

Seasoning sheep and cow horns

If you are only able to obtain freshly harvested horn, it is best stored well away from the house in a well-ventilated dry and cool environment for at least a year before use. Do not keep fresh horns in plastic or polythene bags as they will sweat in the mini climate; use paper or hemp sacks or simply make a pile if space permits. Flies will be attracted to the bloody core of the horn and will lay eggs, resulting in lots of maggots. Allow the maggots to do their work as they will help to clean the core. Ensure the storage place is well ventilated until the horns have dried and the maggots and flies have disappeared. When the horns have dried, the core can often be removed – this can usually be achieved by tapping the horn on a hard surface, which loosens the dried core. Stubborn cores may have to be removed during the boiling process; the horn expands a little which generally allows the core to be removed from the horn. Occasionally the core can be difficult to remove, and has to be drilled to loosen it. Keep seasoned horns in a dry and ventilated environment such as an outbuilding, brick garage or a timber shed.

Working horn

Sheep and cow horns are complex and difficult to work for several reasons. The principal problem with both sheep and cow horns is that a large proportion is hollow, while the tip section is generally solid. Therefore, the hollow section of horn has to be 'bulked' to make it solid so it can be made into a functional handle. The process of bulking requires specialized equipment to squeeze the horn into a solid form that can then be manipulated and shaped into a handle. Horns with thin walls are difficult to bulk, as the walls are liable to collapse when pressure is applied during the bulking process. Try to obtain horns with thick walls; anything with less than $1/4$in (6mm) thickness is liable to collapse. Generally, the older the animal, the thicker the horn will be, therefore horns from young animals are of little use for stickmakers. The number of farmers keeping older animals is reducing; it is chiefly farmers who breed and maintain rare breeds who keep older livestock.

Very old rams can produce extremely large and curled horns that are difficult to work, although they will have plenty of solid horn. Big is not necessarily best. The illustration shows four sheep horns; the walls on the two horns on the left are

Left: Sheep and cow horn sticks.

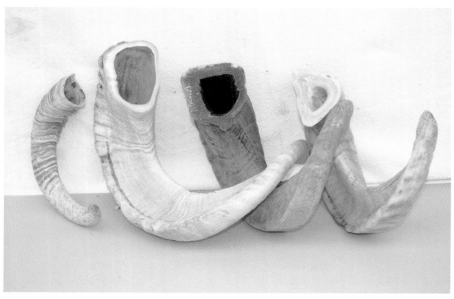
Different wall thicknesses of horn.

too thin to be of use to stickmakers, the dark horn has thicker walls but a large hollow section making it more difficult to bulk, but with care it will make a fine handle. The horn on the right is the best option as it has thick walls and a smaller hollow section, so it will bulk up nicely. However, it does have a deep concave side that must be removed before starting or a crease will form in the horn when it is squeezed in the bulking press.

A common problem with sheep's horns is that they often grow with a concave and convex side, making the bulking process more difficult. If the horn is bulked with a deep concave in it, a crease is likely to form making it unsuitable as a handle. Some concave removal blocks are required to remove the concave from the horn before the bulking process begins. Fortunately, suitable timber blocks can be made with a few carving chisels or rasps, for use in a press. The timber blocks are liable to

crack during regular use but should last for a while. Specialized aluminium blocks can be cast if it is intended to dress a lot of sheep's horn but it is difficult to find anyone willing to cast them as they are fairly uncommon with the result that they are expensive.

As mentioned, horns from older rams often have severe curls in them; the older the ram the more curls they are likely to have. In order to fit the horn into a bulking press or a concave removal press, the curls have to be removed and the horn flattened. A tool that will grip the horn is required to remove as much of the curled section as possible. The tool requires some welding work so it will need an experienced welder/fabricator to make one. It is possible to make a curly-handled stick from a natural horn, but they are difficult to successfully join onto a shank because of their shape.

In order to work and dress sheep and

cow horn, a substantial amount of specialist equipment is required which is quite expensive, especially if you have to get it made for you. Costs can be reduced if you are able to make your own equipment, but few hobbyists have the tools, equipment and materials required to make all of their own implements. Occasionally second-hand equipment becomes available when a stickmaker retires or passes away. Used equipment is sometimes advertised in the quarterly *The Stickmaker* magazine and some online sites. Because hydraulic power is used extensively to bulk and straighten horns in presses and frames, it is important that a competent welder/fabricator completes all the welding on any presses or bulking frames to ensure that the welding will withstand the tremendous pressure applied when using hydraulic jacks to bulk and straighten horns. Working sheep and cow horn requires a considerable amount of patience and time; there is no fast or easy method of dressing a natural horn and making a good-quality and attractive handle. It is advisable to begin learning to dress horns using cheaper 'practice' ones to acquire some experience of manoeuvring the material before using more expensive and scarce horns. Sheep often fight and butt each other and their horns get bruised, causing the formation of blood blisters. Occasionally the dried blood will show through in the horn, warning that a blister may have formed under the surface. Unfortunately, a blister can suddenly appear without warning and a large blister can ruin what potentially was a good horn because it creates a void that cannot be hidden. If a horn is held close to a bright light, a blood blister can sometimes be seen inside, giving the maker some warning of its existence.

TWELVE BASIC STEPS FOR MANIPULATING, FORMING AND DRESSING SHEEP'S HORN

The following step-by-step guides explain the processes used to manipulate and dress sheep's horns using tried and tested techniques that have been used for many years by experienced stickmakers and are still used by the majority of craftsmen.

Step 1. *Select a suitable horn*
Select horns with sufficient length to make your chosen style of handle with substantial walls and a small opening that can be bulked. To prevent a horn from collapsing during the bulking process, horns with a large hollow section are filled with either or both tapered wooden plugs and tapered steel drifts. Tapered steel drifts are slowly withdrawn as the horn is bulked. A wooden plug can be drilled out as the horn tightens onto it and then re-bulked. This is a slow process that requires care and patience to form a hollow horn into a solid state. Horns with a large hollow section should be your second choice of horn.

Step 2. *Boil the horn*
Submerse the horn in boiling water for about twenty to twenty-five minutes depending on the size; a larger horn will require longer. If a horn remains in boiling water for a longer time, it will soften but will not be harmed. If the horn has a large hollow section, plug it with a piece of timber to prevent the horn from collapsing when fastened into the vice to uncurl and flatten it.

Step 3. *Uncurl the horn*
Using tongs or protective gloves, remove the horn from the boiling water and fasten it tightly into a strong vice.

Uncurling the horn.

Remove the curl using the uncurling tool, slip the tool over the horn and carefully open out the curl. Tie or hold the tool with the horn opened in position for about five minutes until it cools and remains uncurled. The horn should be opened sufficiently to allow it to be placed in the concave removal or bulking press.

Step 4. *Flatten the horn*
While the horn is still warm, place it in a flattening press, use a wooden plug to prevent the hollow section from collapsing, and flatten the horn – do not squash it completely. The heel and nose will be aligned which makes it simpler to fit the horn into the concave or bulking blocks. Allow the horn to fully cool before removing it from the flattening press. The cooled horn will remain in its uncurled and flattened state. Consider uncurling and flattening several horns while having set up the boiling equipment; this can be done in a relatively short period of time.

Flattening the uncurled horn.

Step 5. *Remove the concave from the horn*
If the horn has a deep concave along one side, it has to be removed before the bulking process to prevent a crease from forming. A deep crease will ruin the horn. The principal method of removing the concave works by using the cooler (harder) convex side to push the heated (softer) concave side into the shape of a concave block. The concave side is heated to soften the horn more than the convex side; the stronger convex will push the softer concave into a shaped block. The end result will be that an oval (rugby ball) shape will be achieved in the horn. The concave section of the horn is reheated in stages using an electric hot air gun or gas torch with a small nozzle. It is possible to use a gentle gas flame to heat the concave. Select concave removal blocks that will allow the horn to change into the shape of the block. Aluminium or wooden blocks can be used. Place the heated section of horn into the press and block; monitor the horn as the press is closed to ensure the concave is being pushed fully into the concave removal block.

When the first section of the concave is removed, continue moving along the horn using smaller blocks until all the concave has gone; continue to maintain heat in the concave side to soften the horn and use the convex (harder) side to push the horn into the blocks. When the process is complete, remove any surplus

Removing the concave.

horn making it into an oval shape before beginning the bulking sequence.

Step 6. *Bulking the horn*

Bulking a horn has to be carried out with great care and patience; do not attempt to squeeze too much horn in a single pass or it will tear. Begin by selecting a bulking block that just fits around the horn; keep the free space to a minimum to restrict its movement in the blocks. Use a hot air gun to heat the first section and apply sufficient heat to soften the horn but not too much to burn or scorch it; use the press to compress the horn so it fills the bulking block. With the horn held in the block, heat the next section using the hot air gun. Release the horn from the block and move the next heated section into the block and compress it so that it fills the block. As the size of the horn reduces, use a smaller block and continue the sequence along the neck section. Avoid using a block that is too big; it is important to keep control of the movement within the blocks. Do not try to bulk too much horn at a time as it may tear. It may take several passes to complete the bulking sequence. If a large void has to be closed, use a steel drift or a wooden plug, or the two can be used together to support the walls to prevent it from collapsing. Fill most of the void with a drift and/or a wooden plug; the horn is carefully squeezed onto steel drift and wooden plug. The tapered drift is slowly withdrawn as the horn is bulked, reducing the risk of the wall collapsing and forming a crease. Generally, the wooden plug is trapped in the horn and it will compress under the hydraulic pressure; when the wooden plug will no longer compress, the centre section is drilled out leaving a hole that will close during the following bulking sequence. Continue drilling out the wooden peg and bulking the horn using smaller blocks, until the horn is completely bulked. This is a slow

Starting to bulk the horn.

Forming a straight neck.

Bulking the crown and nose.

process; do not try to rush it by attempting to bulk too much horn at once. A range of different-sized drifts are useful to have but if you have a limited number, wooden plugs can easily be shaped using the offcuts from shanks. It is OK if a small amount of a wooden plug remains in the horn, as it will be drilled out when the shank is joined onto the handle.

Begin bulking at the base of the neck and continue along the crown towards the nose. If a square heel is required, leave a short space at the heel position

before continuing along the crown; leaving a gap will help to form a square heel in the horn. During the bulking process, the horn will form a natural curve and sometimes if bulking is continued along the horn it will wrap around the press, making it difficult to remove from the press. Therefore, if this situation occurs, it is good practice to straighten the curved neck section of the handle in a neck press and block to form a straight neck section before bulking all the crown and nose. Heat the neck section (about 3in to 4in) using the hot air gun and bulk the horn in the neck block to form a straight neck. As well as having a straightened neck, the horn will be easier to manipulate within the press during the process of bulking the crown and nose sections.

Using smaller blocks, continue bulking the crown and nose sections of the handle. Again, do not attempt to squeeze too much horn in one pass, take more passes to avoid tearing. When the bulking is complete, the next step is to shape the horn.

Step 7. *Shape the horn around a former*

Bolt your chosen former firmly onto the base of the bending jig. Position the horn onto the jig and clamp the neck section tightly against the side of the former so it will not move during the shaping process. Also clamp the neck so it fits tightly onto the flat base of the jig. This is important as it helps to maintain the alignment of the handle. Use a hot air gun to heat the first section of the horn to be bent, concentrate the heat on the inside of the bend. Use a strong clamp to pull the hot section of horn onto the former; hold it in place with the clamp. It may be necessary to place a non-slip surface between the clamp and horn to prevent the clamp from slipping off during the shaping process. With the first bend held in place, heat the next section to be bent, again concentrate the

Pulling the horn around the former.

heat on the inside of the horn, pull the heated horn tightly onto the former and hold it in place. The first clamp can be removed. Continue the sequence of pulling the horn onto the former, ensuring that the horn is held tightly against it until the nose section is complete. Before the horn completely cools down, clamp it firmly onto the base plate to keep the heel, crown and nose sections aligned, allow the horn to cool completely in an aligned position. When it has set, remove the cooled horn from the bending jig.

If a nose-in handle is required, the horn may have to be transferred onto a circular or a specially shaped former to form a turned-in nose. Reheat the nose section of the horn and pull it around a suitably shaped former.

Step 8. *Tapering the nose*
If a finer nose is required on a handle, it is advisable to taper the horn and reduce the size. Heat the nose section of the horn and place it into the tapered nose block; place the block and horn into a flattening press and compress the horn inside the tapered block. Allow the horn time to cool before removing it from the press and tapered jig. The nose section of the horn now has a tapered section, ready for making a turned-out nose.

Step 9. *Turning the nose out*
Use a jig specifically designed for turning noses on horn handles. Draw a

mark onto the horn indicating the exact position of where the bend is to be made, making allowances for the thickness of the horn; remembering that a nose should always be about $1/2$in (12mm) above the base of the heel. Clamp the horn onto the jig with the heel securely fastened against a fixed anchor bar so it cannot move in any direction. Bolt a bending pin in the appropriate position on the base plate of the jig to match the (mark) position of the bend. Position several anchor points around the jig to enable a sash clamp to be repositioned during the turning sequence. Tighten a sash clamp onto the nose end of the horn and the first anchor point of the jig. Gently heat the inside portion of the bend, keep the heat concentrated on the point of the bend. Apply slight pressure onto the clamp and keep heating the horn until it begins to move, turn the nose as far as possible. (Do not overheat the horn.) Allow the horn to cool and set before releasing and repositioning the clamp onto a different anchor point. With the sash clamp repositioned, reheat the horn on the inside line and apply pressure until it begins to move around the bending pin. Repeat this sequence until the horn has been turned sufficiently around the bending pin to form a turned-out nose. It may be necessary to align the turned-out nose with the crown and heel during and on completion of shaping the nose.

Turning the nose.

Step 10. *Align the handle*
As a result of shaping the nose, it will probably be necessary to realign the handle and fine-tune the shape, as it may have gone out of the desired shape during the nose-turning procedure. Gently heat any section that requires fine-tuning and use clamps or a vice to reposition or refine the shape; allow the horn to cool and set. To align the heel, crown and nose of the handle, gently heat the horn and place it in a flattening press. It may be necessary to use tapered wedges to align the nose with the crown and heel. Compress the flattening press onto the horn, ensuring all the components are aligned perfectly and allow it to completely cool before removing it from the press.

Step 11. *Dress the horn*
With the handle shaped and aligned, begin dressing the horn using a range of rasps, files and abrasives. Remember to leave sufficient material to allow for fitting and jointing the handle onto the shank and most importantly keep the handle components aligned and balanced. Use rasps with care as they can make severe marks in the horn that can be difficult to remove. Initially concentrate on the inside line of the handle; when satisfied with the line and shape of the inside line, complete the rest.

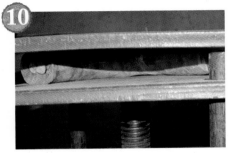

Align the handle in a flattening press.

The handle and shank jointed.

Step 12. *Join handle to shank and finish the stick*
Use a jointing method of your choice to fasten the handle onto a shank, ensuring that they are aligned and the joint is close-fitting before setting and gluing. Allow the adhesive to completely set before finally dressing the horn. Complete the dressing using fine files and a range of abrasives to make a smooth transition between the handle and shank. With the joint marriage completed, dress the rest of the handle and prepare it for your choice of finish.

Fit and glue a ferrule onto the tip of the shank, remove any loose bark and smooth off any protrusions caused by offshoots. Use a sanding sealer to seal the shank. Check the complete stick to ensure there are no unwanted marks or defects before applying your final finish to the handle, shank and ferrule.

MAKING A CARDIGAN STICK

Use the methods and techniques described earlier to select, bulk and flatten the horn. A short piece of fairly bulky horn can be used to make this handle.

Step 1. Bulk up the horn. Leave sufficient material to make the heel and crown on the handle.

Step 2. Clamp the horn onto the bending jig. A former designed for making a cardigan handle is used to shape the horn. Heat the horn using a hot air gun.

Step 3. Pull the horn onto the former ensuring that the heel is held tightly against it. Heat the horn using a hot air gun, concentrate the heat on the inside line.

Step 4. Continue to pull the crown of the horn onto the former, maintain the heat using a hot air gun.

Step 5. Use a sketch of a cardigan handle to compare with the shape of the horn. Dress the horn so that its shape is similar to the sketch.

Step 6. Cut away any surplus material from the handle and shape it using files and rasps, avoid cutting deep marks into the horn.

Step 7. Use an offcut from a sheep's horn to make a thin slice to form a cap over the curved nose of the handle. The slice can be cut from the discarded horn using a sharp hand or band saw. Ensure that the sides are flat and smooth so that it will adhere to the horn with a strong epoxy adhesive. Gently heat so it will bend tightly onto the handle, secure the slice firmly in position using a shaped block to hold the cap until the adhesive has fully set.

Step 8. Carefully shape the cap using files and abrasives so that it fits perfectly onto the horn. Begin the final shaping of the handle with the cap in place.

Step 9. Prepare the handle for jointing onto the shank. An angled joint is used with a dowel cut into the shank.

Step 10. The handle is glued onto the shank and held firmly in place until the glue has set.

The bulked horn.

Clamp the horn onto the jig.

Pull the horn onto the former.

Continue pulling the horn onto the former.

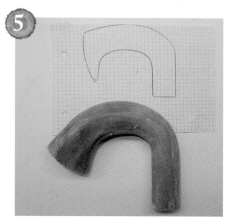

Compare the shape with a sketch.

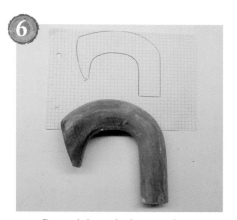

Cut and dress the horn to shape.

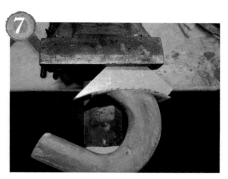

Glue a thin strip of horn to form a cap.

Shaping the capped horn.

The handle prepared for jointing.

The handle glued and held in place.

The finished stick.

Step 11. With the handle attached to the shank, it is carefully dressed so that it merges, making a smooth transition between the two components. The handle and shank are completed and finished. A brass ferrule is fitted onto the tip of the shank.

MAKE A SHEEP'S HORN HARE

This head was carved using a combination of small carving chisels and rotary burrs. If burrs are used, take care as they can quickly remove too much material, but they are useful for making the gentle curves around an animal's head.

Step 1. Use a short piece of surplus horn that has been kicking around in your spares box. Bulk the horn and shape it to form the head and neck around a suitable former.

Step 2. Draw the outline of the head onto the horn; the drawing stands out better when the horn has been painted white. Drill a small hole to mark the position of the eyes; this is used as a datum point throughout the carving sequence.

Step 3. Begin to carve out the details of the ears, nose and cheeks; leave the high points until later. Using the eye sockets as datum points, carve both sides of the head so the features match on each side. Carefully take away any of the lowest points of the carving, leaving the high points until last. This helps to define some of the finer details.

Step 4. Carve out the space between the ears along the top of the head. Note how the eye sockets protrude slightly as the lower points are removed during the carving sequence.

Step 5. Select a suitable pair of glass eyes. Carefully enlarge the eye sockets to fit the eyes using a small rotary cutter. Check that the eyes are a good fit but do not fix them at this stage.

Step 6. Cut an angled joint on the handle and drill out a hole to fit a dowel/peg joint. Then begin the

Use a short piece of surplus horn.

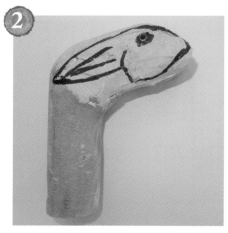

Draw the outline of the hare onto horn.

Start carving the outline of the hare.

Carve the outline of the ears.

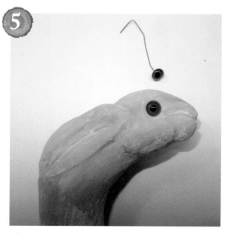

Cut out the eye sockets, check fit of eyes.

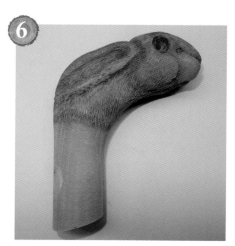

Begin pyrography work.

Make an angled dowel/peg joint.

Glue the head onto the shank.

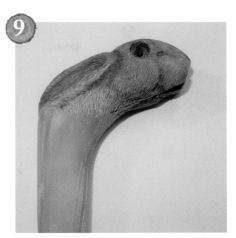

Dress the horn to merge with the shank.

Stain the fur and fit the eyes.

Lighten the colour of the stain.

The finished hare.

pyrography work. Do not use too much heat when carving sheep's horn as it burns very easily; it is advisable to test the temperature of the nib on a waste piece of horn.

Step 7. Choose a seasoned and straightened shank. Make a dowel/peg on the shank or use a turned dowel. Cut the angle on the shank to match that made on the horn handle. Check the fit and alignment of the joint.

Step 8. Mark the handle and shank to show the best position of the joint. Glue the joint together ensuring that the fit and the alignment of the handle and shank are perfect. Hold the assembly firmly until the glue has fully set.

Step 9. When the glue has set, dress the horn until it merges with the shank to form a smooth, clean joint. Complete any pyrography on the handle neck. The fur can be taken to the joint or left slightly short; it is a personal choice.

Step 10. Apply a stain to the fur; the stain will help to highlight the fur when the handle is finished. If the initial colour is too severe, surplus stain will be removed later with a fine abrasive.

Step 11. The dark stain has been lightened but is sufficient to highlight and give some depth to the fur of the hare. Fit a ferrule and complete the stick.

Step 12. The finished hare.

MAKING A HORN HANDLE EAGLE

Step 1. Bulk up a short piece of sheep's horn to make a solid piece and bend it around a former to make the basic shape of an eagle's head and neck.

Step 2. Use a sketch or a photo; adjust the scale of the image to make a template of an eagle and copy the outline of the eagle's head onto the shaped piece of horn. Highlight the position of the eyes that will be used as datum points for shaping the head.

Step 3. Begin to remove surplus horn using carving chisels, rasps or rotary cutters to form the outline of the head. Drill a pilot hole and then enlarge the eye sockets to suit the size of the eyes you intend to use.

Step 4. Continue shaping the head and beak and begin adding detail to the bird's features.

Step 5. With the outline shape complete, smooth off the surface in readiness to add the feather details using a pyrography tool. A smooth surface is essential to obtain a good result with pyrography.

Step 6. Prepare the handle for fitting a tapered nickel collar. Cut a rebate onto the neck to suit the collar.

Step 7. Check the fit of the collar to ensure it is a perfect fit onto the rebate. Dress the neck so that it merges smoothly with the collar.

Step 8. Use a fine pen or pencil to draw the outline of the feathers onto the handle. Drawing the feather shapes and sizes is advisable before burning the details with the pyrography tool.

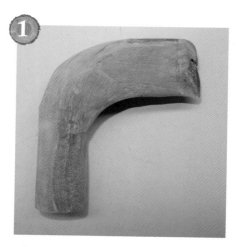

Bulk and shape a piece of sheep's horn.

Draw the outline of the head onto the horn.

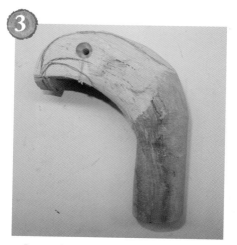

Begin shaping the outline of the head.

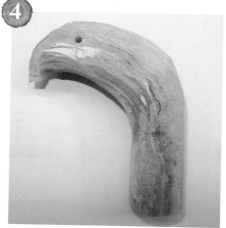

Continue shaping the head and improving the details.

Smooth the surface ready for pyrography.

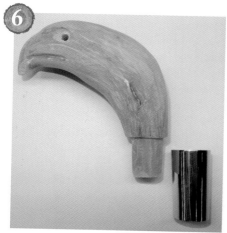

Cut a rebate on the neck for a collar.

Check the fit of the collar on the neck.

Draw the feather details onto the horn.

Start burning the feathers with a pyrography tool.

Use a wire brush to clean the pyrography.

Apply a dark base coat to the head.

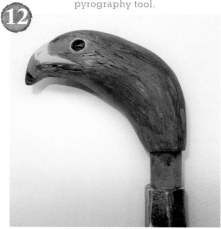

Build up the feather colouring.

Carefully continue with the colouring.

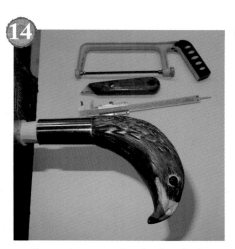

Cut a rebate onto the shank to fit the collar.

Glue and hold the collar onto the neck.

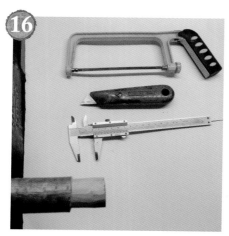

Cut a rebate on the shank to fit the ferrule.

Fit a ferrule onto the tip of the shank.

Finish and complete the eagle stick.

Step 9. Use a pyrography tool with a sharp nib to cut in the feather details on the horn. Highlight the upper and lower sections of the beak and the fine feathers around the eyes.

Step 10. The pyrography pen leaves tiny amounts of burnt horn debris in the base of the lines cut with the nib. Use a stiff wire brush to clean out the debris in readiness for colouring the eagle head.

Step 11. Fit the eyes using an epoxy putty, shape the eye sockets and eye lids. Use a dark paint as a base colour for the head; the dark paint will give the final colouring some depth.

Step 12. Build up the under feather colouring to the head, beak and neck in preparation for the final coloured finish.

Step 13. Highlight the tips of the principal feathers using gold paint. Carefully apply different shades of brown paint to the feathers taking care that the dark base paint shows, giving the feathers some depth.

Step 14. Cut a rebate onto the selected shank to suit the tapered collar using a few basic tools. The collar must be a neat and tight fit; ensure the handle, collar and shank are aligned.

Step 15. Glue the collar onto the handle and secure it in position until the adhesive sets.

Step 16. Cut a rebate onto the shank for a ferrule. The collar and ferrule can be glued onto the shank at the same time.

Step 17. Fit a ferrule onto the tip of the shank.

Step 18. With the head, collar, shank and ferrule fitted and glued together, apply a finish of your choice and complete the stick.

MAKING A COW HORN MARKET STICK

Step 1. Select an appropriately sized horn around 12in to 14in long, with reasonably thick walls. Cow horns generally have a large hollow section that needs supporting to prevent it from crumpling and folding a crease in the horn during the bulking procedure. Use a combination of steel and wooden drifts to support the internal horn. The bulking process follows the same technique as sheep's horn, although it is essential to just move a little at a time to avoid collapse; withdraw a drift a little at a time to maintain support of the horn during bulking.

Step 2. When the horn has been successfully bulked, fix it onto a bending jig, heat the horn using a hot air gun and pull it into shape around a former. Again, move the horn a little at a time as cow horn has a tendency to delaminate during bulking and bending if it is moved too severely.

Step 3. Continue shaping the horn. Remove it from the bending jig and begin to dress the horn handle using rasps. If there are signs of delamination apply thin superglue, which will help to stabilize the horn.

Step 4. Shape and dress the horn to obtain its final shape.

Step 5. Cut an angled joint onto the neck of the horn handle. Make a dowel on the shank with a matching angle and glue the handle onto the shank.

Step 6. When the adhesive has set completely, dress the horn ensuring it merges perfectly onto the shank. Cut the shank to length and fit a ferrule onto the bottom tip.

Select a suitable cow horn.

Pulling the horn around the former.

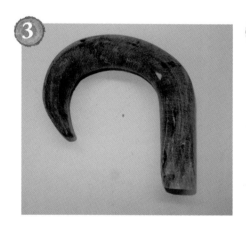

Begin dressing the horn.

Continue dressing the horn.

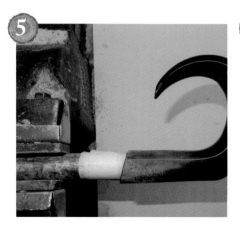

Make an angled joint.

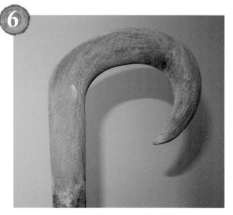

Ensure the joint between the handle and shank merge.

Step 7. Dress the horn and shank until a smooth surface is achieved on all the surfaces. Check that there are no defects such as file or rasp marks on the handle or shank. Fit a ferrule if the length of the stick is known.

Step 8. Polish the horn and shank using rotary mops in readiness for a finish of your choice. Complete a final check for any defects or flaws before applying the finish. The stick is complete.

The stick is ready for varnishing.

Complete the dressing sequence.

MAKING A SHEEP'S HORN CROOK WITH COLLIE DOG

This type of horn handle is more difficult to make because the nose of the handle is substantially larger than the heel, making it more difficult to bulk. A large horn is required to get sufficient material to make the heel, crown and a decorated nose. Horns of the size and quality needed are becoming more difficult to acquire. The horn is bulked using the same procedure as described earlier, although larger bulking blocks may be required to form the larger nose section.

Step 1. Select a large horn and bulk it until it is solid. Fasten the horn onto a bending jig, heat and pull it around a former to obtain the basic shape of the crook.

Step 2. Use photos or drawings to make a cardboard pattern of a collie in its alert position. Draw the outline of the dog onto the wide section of horn that will also form the nose of the crook.

Step 3. Drill a small pilot hole through the horn at the point under the dog's tail and just inside the turn of the crook's

nose. The hole is used as a datum point for carving both sides of the collie dog; all measurements are taken from the hole.

Step 4. The shape of the collie dog and the outline of the crook are defined by removing most of the surplus horn. The horn is reheated and pulled around a former to ensure a satisfactory shape is achieved before the carving commences.

Step 5. With most of the surplus horn removed, an outline of the collie dog's legs and back is drawn onto the outer edge of the handle as a guide prior to carving.

Step 6. Begin the carving by defining the outline of the legs and body, leaving the high points until last. Sharp wood carving chisels or rotary cutters can be used to outline the dog's legs and belly.

Step 7. The legs of the collie have been re-drawn to make them more realistic. A hole is drilled beneath the dog's belly, which is used as another datum point to ensure both sides of the carving are balanced.

Step 8. Continue carving the collie,

carefully define the under-belly and tail, then detail the legs, hips and ears. Refer to photos of collie dogs, especially in a stalking mode as they can be helpful in producing a realistic pose on the carving.

Step 9. As the carving progresses, continue to dress the crook shape, paying particular attention to the nose section of the crook.

Step 10. With the collie shape and the crook defined, the handle is prepared for jointing onto a shank. A 16mm hole is drilled into the handle neck and an angle is cut onto the neck of the crook.

Step 11. Straighten a shank and prepare it for jointing to the handle. Cut a dowel and an angle onto the shank to match the hole and angle of the horn handle. Check that the joint is close-fitting before applying any adhesive.

Step 12. When the adhesive has set, dress the handle so that it merges onto the shank. The whole of the crook handle is now dressed to make a balanced stick. Maintain a straight inside line between the shank and

Select a large horn and bulk until solid.

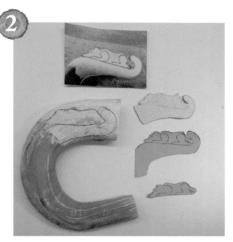

Draw the outline of the dog onto the horn.

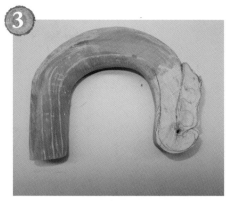

Drill a small hole through the horn.

Re-define the shape before carving.

Draw the profile onto the horn.

Carve out the profile of the collie.

Make a second datum point.

Continue carving the collie dog shape.

Continue to dress the crook.

Cut an angle to make a joint.

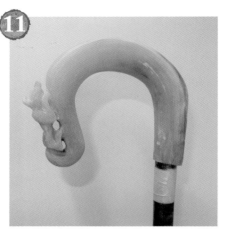

A dowel is made on the shank.

Glue handle onto shank, dress the horn.

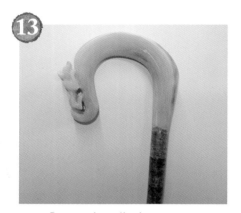

Prepare the collie for painting.

Begin colouring the collie.

Fit the eyes and complete the painting.

The crook and collie dog are complete.

handle, which improves the overall appearance of the stick.

Step 13. Fit a ferrule onto the shank tip. With the handle fastened onto the shank, complete the collie dog and prepare the surface for painting. Smooth off the surface of the crook and shank. Prepare the head for painting.

Step 14. Apply sanding sealer to the shank. Using base paints, start to carefully colour the collie.

Step 15. Fit a pair of small glass eyes

onto the collie dog and then apply the finished coats of paint.

Step 16. When the finished coats of paint and sealers have dried and all the surfaces are satisfactory, apply lacquer or varnish to the complete stick. Several coats may be applied depending on the required finish. When lacquer and varnish has thoroughly dried after several days, the finish can be enhanced by the use of polish or burnishing compounds if a gloss surface is required.

MAKING A LEAPING BROWN TROUT

Step 1. Bulk up a suitable piece of sheep's horn with sufficient material to form the head, body and flat tail of a trout.

Step 2. Heat the horn using a hot air gun and pull it into shape around a former. A wooden former was made to form the curling shape of the leaping trout. The tail section was flattened using the flattening press.

Step 3. Mark out the position of the various features of the trout onto the shaped horn, such as the eyes and various fins. Cut out the mouth of the fish.

Step 4. Carve out all the fins; reduce the amount of horn on the body so the fins protrude a little from the rest of the fish. Use a sharp pyrography blade to burn in the features of the fins and tail. Brush out the debris in the fins and tail using a wire brush.

Step 5. Smooth off the surface of the trout's body with abrasives, then using a small wood carving gouge, cut and form the scales above the lateral line of the fish; this will raise the horn. If the scales are too high, reduce the depth by gently heating them using a hot air gun; also heat a teaspoon and use the curved back of the spoon to flatten the scales. This technique will give the fish an effective appearance. Mount the fish onto a shank and merge the handle to make a smooth transition.

Step 6. Fit the eyes and prepare the handle for painting. Paint tiny white spots above the lateral line and carefully put a spot of red or black paint onto the white background to replicate a brown trout. The natural colour of the horn was used for the majority of the body, tail and fins.

Step 7. Finish the stick, fit a ferrule and use several coats of lacquer or varnish to complete.

Step 8. The picture shows an experiment to mount a trout by the tail following a request from a client.

Bulk up a suitable piece of horn.

Shape the horn and flatten the tail.

Mark the position of eyes and fins.

Carve fins, highlight with pyrography.

Use a small carving gouge to form scales.

Fit the eyes and paint the spots.

The finished brown trout.

A reverse mounted trout.

Chapter 13
Showing and Competing

Stickmaking competitions are regularly held around the country. Several competitions are arranged by the British Stickmakers Guild (BSG); other competitions are run by stickmaking clubs and organizers of county and agricultural shows, game, country and village fairs. Several stickmakers enjoy the challenge of making sticks for competitions and spend many hours improving the quality and appearance of their sticks to the highest standards in order to beat their fellow competitors. Others prefer not to compete but enjoy displaying their sticks for others to see and admire, while some simply make sticks for pleasure, and perhaps give them to friends and family. A few stickmakers sell their work in order to mitigate the cost of materials and equipment required to make a range of sticks. The popularity of stickmaking on social media sites is rapidly increasing, with many makers posting pictures of their sticks for others to view and comment on. This new phenomenon of publishing pictures online is very helpful, especially for people seeking new ideas and inspiration or simply wanting to learn how to perform a particular task. Most members of these sites are keen to share their knowledge when asked about a particular point; a huge advantage with

these sites is that information is available very swiftly, allowing interested recipients to quickly learn and improve their skills.

There are several stickmaking clubs around the UK where members bring and display their sticks at meetings; generally, the public are able to view and ask club members questions and if interested, are encouraged to join the

club. Most clubs have a programme of events that may include demonstrations and occasionally a speaker will be invited to demonstrate a particular aspect of stickmaking at their club. A few stickmaking clubs collaborate with organizers of local fairs and shows to arrange displays and competitions. These competitions often have their own specific classes and rules, which may

Judging show sticks.

Left:Prizes for stickmaking.

vary from the BSG, so ensure that you are familiar with them before entering any sticks.

The competitions organized by The British Stickmakers Guild (BSG) are open for anyone to enter. Most BSG competitions have fourteen open classes and two novice classes. In larger shows, two additional novice classes and a junior class may be introduced. Points are awarded for first, second and third places and the best in show stick is given three bonus points. Over a season the number of points won by the competitors are added together and the champion stickmaker for the year is the one who accumulates the most points. The same arrangement applies for novice stickmakers; the winners are announced at the BSG annual general meeting. A champion of champions' trophy is awarded annually to anyone who enters a stick that won a best in show during the current year; this prestigious competition is generally held at Chatsworth House in Derbyshire. Competitors must comply with the rules and the judge's decision is always final. Some large county shows often run for two or more days and guild members volunteer to demonstrate their skills and display their sticks, allowing anyone to watch the demonstrations and obtain advice from the experienced stickmakers. The stickmaking competition is held on one of the show days and competitors arrive from around the region, bringing a selection of their prized sticks, which must be in place before a pre-set time and collected following the competition. A judge is appointed by the principal officer of the guild and will generally arrive to assess all the sticks after they have been checked in, so he doesn't know who owns the sticks. Competitors are not allowed to place any identification marks on their sticks so they remain anonymous to the judge. Each stick is

given a unique number that is recorded in the steward's logbook and the judge informs the steward of the winning numbers. A steward is often appointed to aid the judge in taking sticks from the rack, replacing them on the instructions of the judge. A matching stub is kept by the competitor, which is their receipt when it comes to collecting the stick at the end of the competition. Occasionally two judges may be used when a high level of entries is expected. The same principal applies for novice stickmakers who are allowed to compete as novices for two years, after which they must participate in the open competitions. In the national BSG competitions, their rules are issued in the magazine and on their website before the competition season begins. The results are published at the end of the competition season in The Stickmaker magazine. In other competitions, there will be classes and rules to comply with and it is important to ensure you understand them before entering your sticks; there is nothing worse than being disqualified for a simple oversight or trying to enter sticks that do not comply with the classes of the competition. Always check with the event organizer or steward before entering any competition.

In traditional stick shows, as well as the rules to conform with, there are also several classes of sticks. Within each class there are expectations as to the style, design, build and materials used for all the sticks to comply with: ensure that you are aware of these limitations. A judge may disqualify or move a stick that is in the wrong class if it does not meet the criteria set by the organizers.

The majority of judges selected to adjudicate traditional stickmaking in the BSG and large competitions are usually experienced in the craft and understand what standards are expected from the competitors. In some smaller competitions, such a village fairs and

even stickmaking clubs, a local dignitary may be asked to judge a competition; unfortunately they are unlikely to be aware of the standards necessary to comply with traditional stickmaking requirements and will select sticks they like the best, irrespective of the quality and workmanship of other sticks. It is important that all competitors understand that judging any competition is difficult and the winning sticks will not necessarily be the choice of the competitors. In some competitions, classes may include unorthodox and unusual sticks which are very difficult to appraise; the judge is likely to choose the stick that he or she simply likes the best. Undoubtedly, the best judge is the one that chooses your stick and the worst is the person who doesn't inspect and handle all the sticks in the competition (especially yours) before making the winning choices. Some of the better judges will explain to the contestants why and how they reached their verdict after the competition, which can be very informative and useful, particularly for anyone beginning competitive stickmaking.

In traditional stickmaking competitions, failure to meet the basic standards and quality of workmanship will inevitably result in sticks being quickly placed back into the stand as judges will almost always begin by discarding sticks that don't meet the basic expectations, such as if the stick is unsuitable for its intended use due to badly positioned carvings, protrusions, the wrong size and height, or poor workmanship and quality. After a judge has eliminated the sticks that don't meet these criteria and is faced with appraising the remaining sticks that meet all the rules and standards, the next things to look for are the slightest defects. These will include (not in any order) any of the following on the handle or shank; poor alignment of handle and shank, open and uneven joints, scratches, file marks, flat points on handles, brush strokes or runs in the finish, unbalanced sticks, poor shapes, badly fitted or no ferrules, bent shanks, poor overall finish, unrealistic and unlifelike carvings, blemishes in the handle or shank that may be natural defects in the original material. To win a class or a best in show award in a renowned competition requires sticks of the highest calibre and quality with absolutely no noticeable imperfections.

Most competition rules will include the following:

1. The complete stick must be made by the competitor, there have been instances where competitors have obtained a stick (or part of a stick) that has been made by another person and entered in a show under their own name.
2. Pre-formed handles are not permitted as they have not been made by the competitor.
3. The maker's name, initials or any identification mark are not permitted on any part of the stick.
4. The stick must comply with the prerequisite of the class. Non-compliance with any of the above may result in disqualification from the competition.

Some of the standards expected are: all joints must be neat, precise, secure and blend seamlessly between all components; handle size should be in proportion for the class and shank; the handle and shank must be aligned; shanks must be straight, twisted shanks must be in alignment from the tip to the handle; sticks must comply with all the rules of the competition; workmanship, artistry, skill and techniques should be of the highest standard.

A stick must be suitable for its intended use. Carvings should be made to scale and be an accurate likeness of the subject. Always check the rules to determine if a ferrule has to be fitted before entering sticks in a competition. Some competitions do not stipulate if ferrules have to be fitted, which is a contentious issue as some judges are of the opinion that a stick without a ferrule is unfinished while others will accept it, providing the tip has been smoothed off. It is advisable to correctly fit a ferrule if there is any uncertainty with the competition rules.

Appendix: A Tribute to Gordon Flintoft

I was brought up in Glaisdale where Gordon and his family farmed. When Gordon retired from farming he and his wife moved into a bungalow in the village next to my widowed mother. My work took me away from Yorkshire but my wife and I visited my mother and family frequently; it was during these visits that Gordon taught me how to make sticks. I would watch Gordon at work, in his workshop at the top of his garden where he would explain and demonstrate his techniques of stick dressing; I was hooked. Gordon told me 'Thou's got good hands and should be able to make sticks,' so he gave me some bits and pieces to take home and I

began making some wooden walking sticks, which I took back on my next visit. Gordon explained where I had gone wrong and how they could be improved. I always remember him telling me that a simple plain stick is the most difficult to make, as the smallest fault or defect will be visible. Over the years during my visits, Gordon taught me how to work and dress sheep's horn and I learnt how to make a range of traditional sticks using wood and horn. I am deeply grateful for all the advice and help Gordon gave me over many years. Gordon was one of the finest stickmakers in the country and he won many awards at the highest level across the UK. He

was always willing to give help and advice to anyone who would listen and was willing to learn the craft of stick dressing. He wasn't keen on those people who thought they knew it all. He taught many people how to make sticks and several of his students are among the best stickmakers in the country, which is a testament to his ability and willingness to share and pass on his experience and knowledge. I must thank Gordon's family for allowing me to take photos of his sticks; some of his prize-winning sticks are shown in the following gallery. I hope you all enjoy seeing some of the finest sticks made by probably the best stick-dresser I have had the pleasure to know.

Gordon Flintoft; Collie dog on crook.

Gordon Flintoft; Thistle on crook.

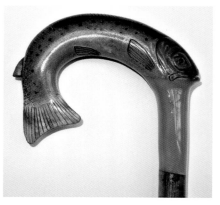

Gordon Flintoft; Trout.

Gordon Flintoft; Bee on thistle.

Gordon Flintoft; Pheasant.

Gordon Flintoft; Four crooks.

Gordon Flintoft; One piece crook and thistle.

Gordon Flintoft; Coloured crook.

Gordon Flintoft; Coloured crook.

Gordon Flintoft; Trio of thumb sticks.

Gordon Flintoft; Trio of leg cleeks.

Acknowledgements

I would like to thank the many stickmakers who have helped me during my stickmaking years. Three very special friends who have sadly died were extremely helpful to me when I was beginning to make sticks; they are Gordon Flintoft, John Penny and George Russell. Both Gordon and John were champion stickmakers; they were great friends as well as fierce competitors and they would both help and advise anyone interested in making show-quality sticks.

George was an experienced stickmaker but did not compete; he was always willing to help anyone wanting to learn the craft. He was able to obtain horns from a local abattoir and would frequently give them to charitable causes for auctioning to help raise funds for the charity. We spent many hours together dressing horn handles and straightening shanks in his workshop; most of his sticks were given away to charities, friends and neighbours.

Gordon was my mother's close neighbour so whenever I visited my mother I would join Gordon in his workshop. He started me off in the craft of 'stick-dressing' as he called it; he gave me projects to complete in between my visits to Yorkshire. It was a while before he paid me a compliment when he told me; 'Thou's improving.' Gordon helped many of us and several of his students have since become great stickmakers. I must thank Gordon's immediate family for allowing me to photograph all of his sticks shortly after his death.

John made sticks in his garage in Torquay; he had an engineering background and every stick he made was precise and exact. His finished sticks were perfect, never a blemish, scratch or unwanted mark were evident in any of his work. He always encouraged novice and experienced stickmakers, many of whom visited him in his workshop where he would give them advice on his methods for making top-quality sticks. I was fortunate to visit John several times at his home.

My thanks to my neighbour Geoff who drew the sketches and diagrams used in this book and a special thanks to my son Richard, who fabricated several of the steel presses used throughout the book. You can tell by the terrible welding the ones that I have altered or made.

Further Information

Rubber Ferrules Team
01279 626900
www.rubberferrules.co.uk
sales@rubberferrules.co.uk
Specialist suppliers of high-quality
rubber ferrules to trade and public. All
types and sizes available for immediate
dispatch.

Robert Wilkinson
Callicrafts
Wellhaven, Bridge of Cally,
Blairgowrie, Perthshire PH10 7JL
01250 886339 (evenings)
Supplier of deer antler.

Dafydd Davies
Fron Villa,
Llanddewi, Brefi,
Ceredigion, Mid Wales SY25 6RS
01974 298566 (evenings)
dafyddsticks@btinternet.com
Handcrafted shepherd's crooks and
walking sticks. Maker of polymer and
horn mouth whistles. Supplier of
stickmaking components.

STS (North Wales) Ltd.
Llanrwst, Conwy LL26 0HU
01492 640664
www.glasseyes.com
Supplier of a large range of glass eyes
suitable for stickmaking.

The British Stickmakers Guild (BSG)
www.thebsg.org.uk
The principal stickmaking organization in
the UK. It has around 2,000 members from
around the world. It publishes four
magazines a year and organizes several
stickmaking shows around the UK.
Provides links to other stickmaking groups.

Martin Hyslop, Director,
The Highland Horn Company Ltd.
Taigh na Corrach, Knockmuir Brae,
Avoch, Easter Ross IV9 8RD
01381 622488
www.highlandhorn.com
Supplier of raw materials to stickmakers.

Keith Pickering
The Stick Man
The Walled Garden, Cleveland Way,
Helmsley, York YO62 5AH
01439 771450
www.thestickman.co.uk
Supplier of stickmaking materials and
teacher of classes for beginners.

Tim Dunning
The End House, Burton Lane
East Coker, Yeovil,
Somerset BA22 9LJ
07585706415
timdunning2013@btinternet.com
Supplier of a wide range of shanks
including knob and block sticks. Timber
also available.

Charlie Walker
Walkers Sticks
www.walkers-sticks.co.uk
Cwalkerssticks@aol.com
Stickmaker and author of *Traditional
Stickmaking* and *Stickmaking – The
Complete Guide*.

John Hallett
JHT Supplies
21 Library Road, Penygraig,
Tonypandy, Wales CF40 1ST
01443 441529
sales@jhtsupplies.co.uk
Supplier of taxidermy materials and a
large range of glass eyes.

Alf Potts
Rerrick Stick Making Supplies
6 Abbey Park, Dundrennan,
Kirkcudbright, Scotland DG6 4QQ
01557 500558
www.rerrickstickmakingsupplies.co.uk
Supplier of a large and varied selection
of stickmaking components and
materials.

Cal Champion
Fern Farm, 30 High Street,
Hinderwell, Saltburn,
Cleveland TS13 5JH
01947 841209 / 07885 751894
Bulking blocks, heel blocks, bulking and
flattening presses.

Index